WHAT THOUGH THE ODDS

HALEY SCOTT'S JOURNEY OF FAITH AND TRIUMPH

BY

HALEY SCOTT DEMARIA

WITH

BOB SCHALLER

To the three women who walked with me throughout the entire journey: Meghan Beeler, Colleen Hipp and my mother, Charlotte Scott.

Authors' Note

To ensure authenticity and veracity, this book was painstakingly researched for more than five years using recorded interviews with teammates, family members, coaches, medical personnel and law enforcement officers; as well as medical records, newspaper clippings, television news coverage, police reports, and a journal Haley Scott kept throughout her journey. Because we felt it was important to remain true to the integrity of the story, this book was documented as best as possible from these sources.

For the sake of storytelling, *What Though the Odds—Haley Scott's Journey of Faith and Triumph* has been written using both present and past tense. Present tense is used to allow the reader to experience the journey as it unfolds. However, past tense is used when necessary for a full reflection and to share a more complete story.

This book is about Haley's journey, her feelings and her recollections. Others who survived this tragedy might have different memories or might choose to focus on different aspects of the story. As all who have lived through any tragedy recognize, coping with loss is a personal experience.

For more information, additional photos, video footage, and to read Haley's blog, please visit www.HaleyBook.com.

Foreword

As a coach for many years, I have witnessed some incredible accomplishments in sports, including many athletes who have defied all odds and overcome all obstacles to achieve success. I have always believed that it isn't what you achieve, but what you had to overcome to achieve, that is most important. Without a doubt, Haley Scott's story told in *What Though the Odds* is the most remarkable feat I have seen. It is a true testimony to her perseverance, her positive attitude, even when it seemed hopeless, and her ability to keep working hard even when it seemed to produce such little results.

Haley Scott was an excellent swimmer from Arizona who matriculated to the University of Notre Dame while I was the head football coach. Her freshman year, coming home from a swim meet against Northwestern University on a snowy night, the bus carrying the Notre Dame swim team slid off the road a few miles from the campus. Of the survivors, Haley was the most seriously injured.

Because of the dire circumstances surrounding Haley's condition, I visited her in the hospital to cheer her up and give her hope. You can imagine my surprise when she was the one who cheered me up. She said she would walk again and swim again. I didn't think that was possible. What Haley proved is that you can accomplish things, even when not everyone believes in you. But, you have no chance to succeed if you don't believe in yourself. It didn't happen overnight, but it did happen. Haley had a total of five lengthy and very serious surgeries, but she prevailed.

Almost two years later, the Notre Dame football team was preparing to play Navy, and the Friday night before the game we received word that Haley Scott had returned to competition. She received an NCAA award for her courage and comeback, which she so richly deserved; and just as predicted, she gave an outstanding acceptance speech. Haley had become an inspiration and a role model for me and thousands of others.

In November 1993, the Notre Dame football team was undefeated and ranked #2 in the country. We were preparing to play the #1 team in the country, Florida State. It would be the first time ever ESPN Gameday would do its show live from a college campus. This game had such nationwide attention that they covered the pep rally on Friday night. The Irish Leprechaun was the emcee and I was waiting to speak, but first he introduced a special guest speaker, Haley Scott. The crowd erupted in pandemonium and her appearance at the pep rally set the tempo for a magical weekend at Notre Dame.

Haley's book, *What Though the Odds*, will inspire, entertain, educate and motivate you, as it has for me.

Lou Holtz
May 2, 2008

1

Swimmers are unique. We spend half our lives underwater, by choice. We spend the other half thinking about how we can improve our time in the water. For those who compete, it is more than a sport, it is a lifestyle. It defines not only our physical shape, but our mental health as well. And when pushed, swimmers rise to the occasion. Coach Tim Welsh told us the first day of practice, "The purpose of Notre Dame Swimming is to pursue athletic excellence with self-discipline and love for one another."

This is why I came to Notre Dame.

Days like today.

It is Thursday night. We are ready to leave Chicago and head back to South Bend, just over a two-hour drive. What a swim meet! I am only a freshman, but I am already holding my own. We just swam against Northwestern University, a Big Ten school with a more established, faster swim team than we have at Notre Dame— at least for now. We made strides tonight. Coach Welsh recruited a very talented freshmen class, and our group is the strength of the team; even the upper-classmen swimmers would say as much. In that regard, I have to imagine we have a pretty unique group of upper-class student-athletes. The ones I talked to knew our incoming class would take spots from them in meets, yet the "older" swimmers felt only excitement to see the program posting better times and results. If there is any resentment from the upper-class swimmers, I have not seen it.

Of course, Northwestern beat us; there was little doubt they would. But even though we lost, it wasn't a blowout. The team and coaches could see we had narrowed the gap on powerful Northwestern. I swam the 100-yard butterfly and the 200-yard freestyle, and did well enough to draw a few compliments from

Coach Tim. As I walked around the pool deck after swimming my last event, Tim pulled me aside.

"You know, your 200 tonight was great, especially in the middle of hard training," he said. "You would do really well at middle-distance."

Normally a compliment like this would be met with a groan. The truth is I have always fancied myself a 50 freestyle swimmer—a "sprinter." I like the shorter "sprint" workouts better than the long- or middle-distance ones. But in reality, I do not have that quick, flat-out speed needed to be a sprint specialist. I was fast enough to get by as a sprinter in high school and with the club team I swam for in Phoenix, but not at the collegiate level. I recognize this and with Tim's confidence, realize I can probably be a pretty good middle-distance swimmer, maybe a great one. I am eager to try, and I am looking forward to swimming the 500-yard freestyle at our next meet.

January is such a great time of year. I have one semester of college under my belt, and everything is even better than I hoped it would be. I mean *everything*: the academics, the swimming, and the social life. Notre Dame has more than lived up to my hopes and expectations; it has become the center of my life. The professors are engaging, and while the school work is challenging, it is also enjoyable. Mostly, it is the Notre Dame community—my friends and teammates—that has stolen my heart. Everything has fallen into place. But we are college girls, so at this age we are still pretty optimistic. Life is good. Plus the swimming went so well tonight.

We are traveling without the Notre Dame men's swimming team today. Unlike the rest of our season, tonight's Northwestern meet was women only. Awesome, we have the bus to ourselves. While we like having the boys around, this is a nice change. In the bus, there is a restroom in the corner on the passenger's side, next to a group of three seats along the back. We feel lucky, without the guys, to have control of the bathroom. Huddled in the back, the boys would taunt us and give us a hard time, so usually we would have to hold it until we got back to Notre Dame.

Tonight, we also get to pick the movie, *Dying Young*, a total chick flick. In it, Julia Roberts plays Hilary O'Neil, who is looking for a change in life and becomes a personal nurse to Victor Geddes

(Campbell Scott). His character is dying of cancer, and they fall in love. It is definitely a tearjerker (case in point: Kenny G is on the soundtrack). This movie would not be allowed within 100 feet of the bus's VCR if we had the boys along. Instead we would have to endure something ridiculously silly like the Chevy Chase movie *Fletch* or a *Seinfeld* marathon; recently, during one six-hour bus trip, the boys played 12 straight episodes. The guys definitely think they run the show on bus trips, but we adore them just the same. There are, after all, a lot of cute guys on our team.

We are traveling, as we always do, in "Dress Code A," meaning we are fairly dressed up. I am wearing my very favorite outfit: a raspberry and black striped knit top and skirt, and my black cowboy boots—a touch of Arizona. I love this outfit. Coach Tim does, too. Even though he lives in South Bend, Tim is a cowboy at heart and often wears his cowboy hat.

Thankfully we brought our Notre Dame swimming parkas, because there are snow flurries as we board the bus for the ride home. Earlier today, it was sunny and relatively warm out. Around 1 p.m., after my 30-minute "loosen-up swim" at Notre Dame's pool, "Rolfs" (short for Rolfs Aquatic Center), I didn't even have to wear a coat as we boarded the bus to leave for Northwestern.

We stopped on the way to Chicago to eat at the Old Country Buffet. I am not big on their all-you-can-eat mashed potatoes buffet, but they do have a good yogurt bar. I'm sort of famous on the team for my love of frozen yogurt. Now on the way home, Christy Cook, our team's manager has picked up pizza, bread and salad. With that and a chick flick, the bus ride back to South Bend becomes "girls' night out." With Chicago behind us, I debate whether or not I should have a third piece of pizza.

I am content in my environment. I could not have picked a better school to swim at, or a better group of girls to call my teammates and friends. Because I have never liked cold weather, I initially did not consider Notre Dame for college when I was being recruited out of high school. But spring-like temperatures on my recruiting trip to Notre Dame, almost exactly a year ago, made me think that all of the talk about the cold Indiana winters was exaggerated. It wasn't. Now, despite being an Arizona native and seeing the snow blow outside the bus, I know I am in the right place, just where I belong.

Dying Young begins and most of us continue to eat pizza, laugh and gossip, while some of us study. Occasionally, girls shift from the passenger side of the bus, where the movie can be seen, to the driver's side, where they turn on an overhead light to read or study.

I am sitting next to Colleen Hipp, a freshman teammate from St. Louis. Often found behind a camera taking pictures to record our misgivings and late-night antics, Colleen is quiet and incredibly thoughtful. For Christmas last month, she made green-and-red-beaded wreath earrings for every freshman on the team. In her own way, Colleen has made such an impression on everyone in just the few months she has been at Notre Dame. I am enjoying sitting next to her and getting to know her a little better.

Meghan Beeler, an attractive and outgoing freshman from South Bend, moves across the aisle from her seat next to Susan "Scully" Bohdan on the passenger side, to the back row to study. Some of us find this odd, because Meghan doesn't often study on bus trips; she doesn't have to. Her 4.0 grade-point average first semester came easy to her. Meghan is entertaining and funny and people gravitate toward her. At times I wish I could be more like Meghan. I am much more introverted, and I think we are often drawn toward people who have qualities we would like to see in ourselves. Life, or the things that seem important in life to teenage girls, comes easy to Meghan, and I admire her for that.

Standing up to stretch my legs and walk around, I decide to go to the bathroom. With no boys, I can go without being teased. When I come out, Meghan has moved to the back-row window seat on the driver's side, leaving an open seat across the aisle next to Scully.

Scully received her nickname because her three older brothers also swam at Notre Dame and had the same nickname. She is cute but not gorgeous—I am certain we are both described that way—and all the guys really like hanging out with her. Again, I admire that about her. She was the first swimmer I met at Notre Dame last year when she hosted me on my recruiting trip.

I decide to watch the end of the movie next to Scully, who slides over towards the window in the seat where Meghan had just been. Scully kicks her shoes off, and I relax alongside her as we prepare to cry at the end of the movie.

Another freshman teammate, Angie Roby, smiles as she passes us on the way to talk to Meghan. Angie and Meghan are in the same chemistry class, and discuss the following day's quiz, for which both she and Meghan are studying. Angie also lives in my dorm, Lyons Hall, which is the furthest female dorm from the pool. Thankfully, Angie and I, and Amy Bethem, a third freshman swimmer and Lyonite, have bicycles to ride the mile-long trek to the pool. Just last week, it was so cold our damp eye-lashes froze as we rode our bikes from the pool back to our dorm. Then today it was 60-degrees, and now back to snowing. Okay, so maybe South Bend does have strange weather.

Directly in front of Meghan is Lorrei Horenkamp, another freshman and one of my closest friends on the team. When I first met Lorrei last August, she made a big impression on me because we looked so much alike. People mistake us for each other all the time. Yet like Meghan, Lorrei is more outgoing than I am. Once I got to know her, I realized we were similar in many ways, and a connection was made.

Earlier in the year, Lorrei, Meghan and I attended a party at the "Swim House." The Swim House, an off-campus house usually inhabited by senior guy swimmers, often becomes a gathering place for members of the team and their friends. Because Notre Dame does not have a Greek System, a team, club or dorm becomes a second family and social network for students. And swimmers love to socialize. That particular night at the Swim House, Meghan, Lorrei and I had our picture taken in front of a cardboard cutout of the *Three Amigos*, the movie with Steve Martin, Chevy Chase and Martin Short. I had the picture enlarged and framed, and I sent it to Meghan for her birthday over Christmas break. I made a copy for Lorrei and me as well, so each "Amigo" would have one to keep.

One of our senior captains, Shana Stephens, also comes to the back of the bus. She and Meghan talk and laugh, and make plans to go out tonight when we get back to South Bend. Meghan puts on her yellow SONY walkman and listens to music.

In the window seat in front of Meghan, Lorrei continues to read. Right in front of Lorrei is Colleen Hipp, and the seat where I previously sat.

Outside, the snow and wind intensify, and I am thankful that we a.e close to our exit on the Indiana Toll Road. Only a few minutes and we will be back on campus. This geographically unique storm is called a "lake-effect blizzard," which can turn a standard snowstorm into whiteout conditions instantly. Snow has settled on the icy road, and it is well below freezing, some 30 degrees colder than earlier today. The credits for *Dying Young* are rolling, and the theme song "I'll Never Leave You" is heart-breaking and beautiful.

While we are college girls and a movie like this can make us cry, none of us can truly relate to the story. It is difficult to think of death as something tangible in our lives; most of us are too young to have lost anyone close to us. We do not think we are invincible, like some of the guys on the team view themselves, but death is so far distant that it is not on our emotional radar. Despite our innocence, the quiet ending of the movie and the way it portrays such a gentle yet powerful reverence for life, is touching.

Jackie Jones, our other senior captain, stands to rewind the VCR tape. I feel the bus move a little to the left, but a moment later we start back to the right. I think we are exiting down the ramp. I crane my neck to look at where we are, but the bus keeps moving to the right. With a quick jerk, we slide and fishtail 180 degrees.

There is no time to think, no time to react, no time to hold on—though that is what our coach yells, "Hold on!" And no time to pray.

The bus slides down an embankment, and several windows, despite their safety latches, inexplicably pop out. Two girls are thrown out of the bus to the ground, through these open windows. A third girl smashes her head into the window support divider, but is saved by the partition from being thrown out of the bus. In another unlikely and unfortunate circumstance, a rear tire catches a cement culvert as the bus slides off the road, flipping the backward facing bus upside down. Because of the slope of the embankment, the bus rolls over onto its roof and—unbeknownst to any of us—on top of two of my teammates, two of my friends. We are just four miles from campus.

Silence. No screaming, no yelling. For a moment we are in shock. Then there are cries. Screams. My only thought is to get off the bus. A teammate asks for help. She is stuck, but I cannot help her, and instead I pull myself through the open window and out into the bitter cold. I try to walk, but I am unable and fall into the snow. Wet snow slaps my cheeks and begins to numb my body. I start shivering. I cannot fathom what has happened, and I should probably be thankful that shock shields me from the grim reality that lies in a heap in, around—and most sadly of all—under this bus, on this Indiana road, in the middle of this winter night just minutes into January 24, 1992.

2

Scully and I are the first two off the bus. She thinks she is the only survivor until she sees me exit from the window we shared. She comes over to ask if I am okay and kneels down to comfort me.

"My back hurts," I say. "Help me up, I want to walk it off."

"No, stay still," she says firmly, cradling my shoulders in her arms, which are warm.

I am on my side, and I heed her order, mainly because I have tried to move and cannot.

"I can't feel my legs," I tell her.

There is little noise from the Toll Road. Passing cars and trucks drive by, and then pull over to offer assistance. Traffic slows down going the other direction. Headlight beams scatter and pierce the air in a chaotic way. Navy blue and gold swim parkas, books, pizza boxes and shoes are scattered in the snow. There is more movement as other teammates are helped or pry themselves from the bus. But I am oblivious to it all.

"I want to go back to Arizona," I tell Scully. "I am so cold."

Lying in the snow, freezing, I focus on two things: my jaw, which has locked up; and my legs, which in a different way, have locked up as well.

"Scully, get this gum out of my mouth," I order through clenched teeth. I am afraid if I cannot chew, I will choke on it.

Scully swipes it out and then, as though she can read my mind, tries to ease my fears by telling me my legs are probably numb from lying in the snow. I believe her. Of course, that makes sense. I am lying with what is really just a big ice pack underneath me, so my legs are numb.

I notice Lorrei standing over me, staring blankly.

"Lorrei, my back hurts," I say, half as a complaint and half as a plea for help. She stands there for a moment, eyes glazed, looking through me, and then walks away without saying a word.

There is more cold and more people walking around. I hear their voices, but I am not listening, nor can I decipher what they say. I just hear noise and every so often, Scully's voice telling me to stay still, and that help is coming. I see very little besides her face, darkness and the silhouettes of shadows moving around. My body continues to shake and I am irritated that I cannot get up and walk around to stay warm. We remain like this for over an hour, but it seems much longer.

Kevin Kubsch, a state trooper, arrives with a paramedic. I also see our Assistant Coach, Randy Julian. Trooper Kubsch and the paramedic carry a backboard down the embankment, and everyone lines up to move me. I hear words of caution about moving me, concerns about my back and further injury, but their words are hollow to me. My only thought is how grateful I am to be one of the first ones taken away; I will be warm soon inside an ambulance.

"One! Two! Three!" They shout and move me in unison to the board, then pick me up onto a stretcher. Randy's arm or wrist looks broken, but he still helps to lift me.

"Oh God, I can't feel my legs!" I yell, as though I just noticed. Randy's eyes open wide.

I am put into an ambulance. The panic I feel about my legs gives way to gratitude for being the first one taken to the hospital. But I also feel guilty. What about the girls who are really hurt? There are girls who have concussions and probably others with broken bones. Why are they taking me first? My confusion is short lived as thoughts rush through my head. I am completely in the moment, my mind in shock.

Scully does not come with me. Instead Cyndi Safford, a senior, climbs into the ambulance and sits next to me. We do not drive very fast because of the snow.

"I can't feel my legs," I tell Cyndi over and over. "I can't feel my legs and my back really hurts."

"You will be okay," Cyndi assures me.

I tell Cyndi I need her to call my parents.

My parents. My poor mother. They will be worried, especially if they hear about this from a police officer or someone from the hospital. I need someone I know to call them.

"Cyndi, you have to call my parents," I plead.

"Let's just get to the hospital," Cyndi says. "It's late, we can wait until morning."

"No," I tell her, "I need you to be the one who calls them. I know if you call them, they will come."

I tell Cyndi my parents' phone number and ask her to repeat it back to me several times, until I am sure she knows it. She promises she will call them when we get to the hospital. This eases my mind a bit, but I still ask her repeatedly to recite the phone number, just in case she forgets.

There is another swimmer in the ambulance with us. I do not know who it is, but I hear they are taking her to a different hospital, St. Joseph's. Most of the swimmers will go there. But first the ambulance stops at Memorial Hospital of South Bend. My stop. I wonder, although only briefly, why I am being taken here. But really, I am just glad that I get dropped off first. Despite the blankets draped over me, I am still freezing, shaking and anxious to get inside, hoping I will warm up.

In the emergency room, people introduce themselves to me, and ask if I am all right. My response is always the same, "My back hurts and I can't feel my legs." I do not remember their names, but their faces all register the same sympathetic look. No one has an answer they want to tell me or that I want to hear, and therefore no one says much. I get several pats on the arm and concerned smiles.

A nurse checks my temperature and whispers, "95.5 degrees—hypothermic."

They need to take off my wet, cold clothes and apply direct heat on my body.

"We need to cut them off," someone says.

"What? No, I'll just take it off," I tell them. "I love this outfit."

The ER nurse looks at me sympathetically, not sure what to say.

"Will it hurt more if I try to take it off?" I ask.

The nurse now knows what to say, "Yes."

"Cut it off."

Magically, scissors, or some cutting apparatus, appear and I close my eyes as the nurse cuts up the front of my favorite outfit.

"It is a good thing I am not modest," I think to myself as I lay here in my underwear. Another random thought pops into my head as I think of some of my non-swimmer friends who won't change their clothes in front of me. I always found this odd, but then realized that swimmers, by nature, do not tend to be very modest people. We spend half our lives in bathing suits smaller than undergarments.

Piece by piece, my attire is deconstructed. I am asked to take out my earrings and notice that one is missing. My heart sinks. I love these earrings: interlocking blue and gold NDs.

"We'll keep this for you," a nurse says, taking the remaining earring from me.

"Why bother," I think, disappointed. But then I am distracted by the next question: "Do you wear contact lenses?"

"Yes," I reply. And I remove them too. If anything was remotely clear to me before, it now all becomes a blur.

They cover me with heated blankets and the warmth feels good on my skin. However, the blankets do little to stop my shivering. My whole core is shaking. I am told I am to be taken for an MRI to assess the damage to my back. Still on the gurney, I am wheeled away to a room where I am placed extremely carefully on a flat, narrow and cold surface. So much for the blankets. The nurse, Jeff, who preps me for the MRI, is a good-looking guy. He doesn't say much, but he has kind eyes and a nice smile. As he lines me up on the MRI table, I roll slightly to one side and vomit all over him. Our eyes meet for a second before he tells me that it is no big deal. He smiles and asks if I am all right.

"Crap," I think to myself, "if I'd have known I was going to throw up I would have eaten that third piece of pizza!" I am not aware that my thoughts and actions are signs of shock.

As I move slowly into the cold, loud MRI tunnel, my body is still shivering. I am as cold now as I was outside in the snow. I try to take deep breaths to relax my frozen, shaking body, but it does not work.

Thankfully, the test is not long and as I am taken back to the emergency room, the heated blankets are over me once again. Finally, I start to warm up.

In the ER, I see my first familiar face: Dr. Klauer. Dr. Roger Klauer works at Memorial Hospital, but he also leads our swim team in mental imagery. I wonder how he got here so quickly, but I am glad to see him.

Dr. Klauer does not say hello or ask me how I am, he just leans down and whispers in my ear, "No swelling, no bleeding, no pain."

I give him a confused look.

"No swelling, no bleeding, no pain," he says again. "Keep repeating that over and over to yourself until your body believes it." Dr. Klauer specializes in rehabilitation, and some of his practices border on alternative methods. I heed his message and focus on this positive mental picture.

"No swelling, no bleeding, no pain," I repeat to myself over and over. While it does not necessarily take away the pain, it is helpful to have something on which to focus.

"The first MRI is inconclusive," a doctor tells the nurse, or perhaps he is talking to me. I had been shaking too much and the images are unreadable.

By the time they wheel me back to the MRI room, I have warmed up significantly. But the room is cold again. I wonder to myself, or maybe aloud—but no one answers me—why I can't keep the blankets on during the MRI. If it can take pictures through my skin, can't it take pictures through the blankets? The cold MRI tunnel replaces my heated-blanket cocoon.

Better news this time. The second MRI gives the doctors hope that perhaps my spinal cord is not severed. However, the results are hardly conclusive; once again the images are less than perfect, due in no small part to my continued shivering.

This time the doctor addresses me directly. Dr. Dave Halperin introduces himself as the emergency room doctor on call, and explains the situation. My vertebrae are shattered at levels T-8, T-9 and T-10, the center of my back. Normally square, my vertebrae have been crushed to the shape of a piece of pizza, triangular. Because I said I walked off the bus, and with the MRI data, they have reason to believe my spinal cord was not completely severed, which would have meant instant, permanent paralysis. However, the paralysis I am experiencing might still be permanent *if* the spinal cord was irreversibly damaged from the pressure of the crushed vertebrae *or* from the swelling of the spinal cord tissue.

Dr. Halperin asks if I understand. I nod my head. I think I do, but I cannot possibly.

He continues to explain that while surgery on a traumatized spine is difficult and risky, to operate is the only way to relieve pressure and swelling of the spinal cord. Emergency surgery might not help, and there is always the chance it could do more damage, but I will need to have my spine operated on at some point. The bones are broken and the longer we wait, the less chance I have to walk again.

Dr. Halperin looks at me, as though I am supposed to decide. Thoughts rush through my head and I think back to when my mom had back surgery five years ago. My only memory is that she was terrified. But for some reason I am not scared.

"Well, what are we waiting for?" I ask. "Let's do it."

As though by magic, or perhaps because I have no concept of time, all of a sudden I am holding the consent form above my face and I sign it. "Good thing I am 18 years old," I think, technically considered an adult. And it is a good thing I am conscious, because without consent, they will not operate.

I wonder if they can read my signature. It is so messy, almost illegible.

It is 4 a.m., and I am headed into emergency surgery in South Bend, Indiana. It is not the middle of nowhere, but it is not a major medical center either.

Dr. Thomas Keucher, the neurosurgeon on call, who has been awakened in the middle of the night, attempts to stabilize my spine during a four-hour and forty-minute operation. Dr. Keucher cleans out pieces of bone that have broken off from my compressed and fractured vertebrae. He takes a bone graft from my hip, and extracts a portion of my tenth rib. He attaches two 8-inch metal rods to my spine to aid in support and fusion.

When I wake up in the recovery room, Dr. Klauer is sending me more positive messages. "No swelling, no bleeding, no pain," he repeats again and again.

Missy Conboy is here. The young, auburn-haired assistant athletic director at Notre Dame says my parents are flying in and should be here before noon. She then asks me if there is anyone else I need her to contact. I ask her to call Nancy Martin, my best friend since childhood, who attends St. Mary's College across the street from Notre Dame. Missy tells me she will take care of it.

Shawn, my recovery room nurse, is adamant that she sees my toe move. She wants to call Dr. Keucher.

"It could have just been a reflex," someone tells her, "as opposed to regaining function." This is debated for almost an hour, as no one else has seen any movement from my toes.

Shawn finally decides to call Dr. Keucher. He had gone home after operating for some well-deserved rest. Upon hearing the news that I moved my toe, but then lost function again, he is hopeful that it is only a blood clot preventing signals from being sent to my lower extremities. A clot might not show up on any additional X-rays or scans; he will need to operate again to find and remove it.

I am too groggy to sign a second consent form. With my parents en route to South Bend, someone from the hospital calls my brother, Stephen, in Atlanta. He is talking to his girlfriend, and the operator does an emergency break-through to reach him. Stephen authorizes the second surgery, and at 11 a.m., Dr. Keucher and I return to the operating room. I am barely alert and do not fully understand the importance of this exploratory surgery.

The second surgery is different from the first: shorter and unproductive, but not without risk. Dr. Keucher tries to find out why I lost movement. He finds nothing; again he confirms that my spine is not severed, which is good, but he finds no blood clot either. There is nothing tangible to indicate that my toe's movement was anything more than a reflex.

Faces look different when I come out of surgery. Something is wrong, and while everyone is saying positive things, I can deduce that they are concerned. I have heard "paralysis" a couple of times, but I do not believe that is possible. My back is so tight and stiff. If I could move, and I cannot, I would be afraid to touch it for fear of increasing the pain. My legs are numb and I have no feeling in them or in my feet.

A tall, white-haired man walks to my bedside, gently touches my arm and introduces himself.

"Hi Haley," he says. "I am Father Malloy."

The President of the University of Notre Dame. He had been in

Washington, D.C. that morning, but flew back to South Bend as soon as he heard about the accident.

"May I pray with you?" he asks.

I am in awe of this humble and kind man. "But I am not Catholic," I reply.

"That doesn't matter," he says calmly. "May we still pray?"

I nod my head "yes" and tears fill my eyes.

He begins, "Heavenly Father…"

3

My poor mother.

The phone rings in my parents' house. My mother, Charlotte, hears it and wakes up, thinking she has heard the clock alarm. She looks at the clock, 11:38 p.m., and realizes the noise is from the phone. She looks over at my father, Steve. All she can see is my father's back. From his posture, she knows this is not a call they want to get. They have been married for 25 years and know each other that well. These middle-of-the-night phone calls are often a parent's worst nightmare, the kind of call that punches you in the stomach and takes your breath away; one that makes you strain to make sense of the nonsensical information coming through a phone receiver in the middle of the night.

My mother is slowly waking up, but her nightmare is only beginning. She walks around their bed in our Phoenix home to look at his face. "What's wrong? What's going on?" she mouths. My father is getting information, so he is not responding in kind. He is listening because he needs to, and when it is time, he will ask questions. My father holds his hand up in a "stop" position. He might as well: time has stopped for my parents. From this point on, there will be life before the accident and life after the accident. More lives are changing.

Cyndi Safford, the teammate and friend who took my plea to heart, is telling my father what she knows, which is only what she experienced herself, and heard from me. My mother studies my father, gleaning details from his expressions and tone. She knows this is not good. He scribbles a number on a pad.

"Haley wants you to come," Cyndi tells my father.

"We are on our way," my father says.

My mother's hand goes over her mouth as my father hangs up the phone. Her stomach sinks. She is breathless. I love this complex woman with all my heart. She is nurturing and kind, runs a preschool and is great with kids. I am more like my father than my mother, but I am her first daughter, and our bond is strong. As complex as she is to me, I am that and more to her. Yet she never gives up trying to understand me.

"Haley has been in an accident," Dad tells her. "We can't talk to her."

My mother has the same questions my father is thinking or has just asked, and he has no answers. "Haley," he says again, "has been in an accident. The team was returning from a meet in Chicago and there was a snowstorm. Haley is in the emergency room. They won't let me talk to her or the doctors. I have to call back when they have a diagnosis.

"That was Cyndi on the phone. She can hear Haley talking and all she knows is that Haley cannot feel her legs. She rode in the ambulance with Haley and said that Haley made her memorize our phone number and promise to call us. Haley wants us to come."

My father calls his stepmother, Carolyn, to watch my little sister, Mary Frances, who is just 14 years old. My mother calls Mindy, her assistant at the preschool, and then Barbara Gallagher, the wife of my father's law partner. They share no details except there is an emergency in South Bend, and they will call with more information tomorrow or the next day.

My mother goes to quickly pack. In our garage she finds a small old suitcase with my initials embroidered on it, her way of being closer to me until she gets here. Her mind is racing with what is happening to her daughter in South Bend: where is she and what is she feeling, is she scared and how much pain is she in? My mother throws in a sweat outfit her staff gave her for Christmas last month; it has an apple on it, and reads "DELICIOUS" down the sleeve. She has just two small carry-on bags, one each for my father and herself.

My mother starts to walk into Mary Frances' room, the one Mary Frances and I shared as young girls, and stops. Mom wants to look at her peaceful expression one more time before she wakes her. Her youngest child is going to have her life interrupted; she is going to lose some of her childhood innocence, because when a family's life is hit by tragedy, the burden is borne by everyone. And in this case, it is a girl in her early teenage years, when the support system, particularly the mother, is needed more than ever.

She gently wakes Mary Frances, who puts a coat on for the trip to our grandmother's home. Mary Frances goes to my parents' room and sits next to my father as he calls the airport to book a flight to South Bend. My mom is in the kitchen on the other phone line calling family members, including my brother who lives in Atlanta. He too, my mother knows, will have his world rocked. But Stephen is almost 24; he has graduated from college and has entered the business world. He will be better able than young Mary Frances to handle the emotional upheaval our family is about to experience.

My father finally gets through to the emergency room and Dr. Halperin, who my dad learns is, coincidentally, a friend of Coach Tim Welsh. My father is told that I was shaking so badly from hypothermia that the first MRI could not be read. My father presses for details, and the doctor relents.

"My best guess," Dr. Halperin tells my dad, "is that Haley is paralyzed from the waist down. If the spinal cord is severed, we will let the swelling go down, and we won't do surgery for another four or five days."

The doctor adds that a second MRI will either "confirm my suspicion or we will decide to operate." My mom finds it difficult to pray that her daughter will have to undergo emergency back surgery in the middle of the night. But she knows she must.

Mary Frances hears my father relating this to my mother, and her little mouth opens, "No!" she screams, "Not my sister. Not Haley!" Her youngest daughter's terrified cries tear at my mother's overly stretched heartstrings.

The 10-minute drive to my grandmother's house is cold, dark and quiet. My mom reassures Mary Frances that she or my father will call soon and…and…what else, my mother thinks, do I tell this little girl? Tears run down my sister's face as she is dropped off in her slippers, her nightgown sticking out beneath her coat.

My parents close their car doors. My father puts the car into drive, and looks straight ahead.

"This has to be a nightmare," he says. "And I hope we will wake up soon."

The airport's lights are bright. My mother has to squint and she wonders if people can see the fear on her face. They pace and wait for their 3:30 a.m. TWA flight at Phoenix's Sky Harbor International Airport, the soonest flight available when my father called shortly before midnight. My father calls the hospital again.

"Your daughter is in surgery," he is told. "She signed the consent form herself."

My father looks at my mother, who connects the dots right away. My mom is even more anxious to see me, and she sadly whispers to herself, "My poor daughter. She knows she is paralyzed."

My parents board their flight to St. Louis, where they will find a connecting flight. They hold hands at times, other times they close their eyes and gather their thoughts alone.

The flight attendant asks my mom if she wants something to eat during the food service portion of the flight.

Shaking, my mother looks at her and says, "I can't imagine ever eating again." The flight attendant quietly moves back another row to offer up an airline meal; ironically similar to hospital food: not something one would choose, but under the circumstances, the best available option. And sometimes you just have to embrace the best available option.

My mother is talking to herself, and to me, in her mind. She fears I am still shivering, still cold.

"I will be there soon, Haley, and hold you, and we will both be warm," she repeats to herself.

My father says aloud, again and again, "I keep thinking, hoping this is a nightmare and I'll wake up soon."

They land in St. Louis, and the airport is cold, another place foreign to them that has no answers. They head to the TWA airline information counter trying to find a faster connection to South Bend. There are no direct flights. They will have to switch airlines, settle for a flight to Chicago, and then "puddle jump" to South Bend.

"My daughter has been hurt," my mother tells the ticket agent with beautiful skin. The woman puts her smooth, dark hand with perfectly painted fingernails on top of my mother's. My mother looks at the two entwined hands, the woman's lovely hands and her own, which are dry and cracked from constant washing at preschool. The agent looks directly into my mother's eyes as she places the tickets in my mother's hands, and in a peaceful, sincere voice says quietly, "Your daughter is in God's hands. She is going to be fine."

An unexpected peace comes over my mother.

My mother does not know that later this morning, Friday, she would have arrived at her preschool to find a surprise 45th birthday celebration. Her staff has gone all out with breakfast, cake and decorations. But plans change. Life changes. Somewhere in the night my parents probably pass the plane carrying the birthday card I mailed her two days ago.

My parents wait for their connecting flight in an airline club lounge. In the pre-business-day calm they start to make phone calls to extended family when the television catches their attention. It is CNN, and they are showing an upside down bus in a blizzard. My mother turns away, while my father steps closer to the television.

"Tragedy at Notre Dame," The CNN anchor reports. "A bus carrying the Notre Dame swimming team overturned in a snowstorm early this morning. Two girls died in the crash."

Pictures of Meghan and Colleen from the university's media guide appear on the television screen.

"Killed in the accident were Meghan Beeler of nearby Granger, Indiana, and Colleen Hipp of St. Louis, Missouri," the anchor continues. "Another teammate is seriously injured and still in the hospital. No details are being released at this time."

Dad and Mom know I am the "seriously injured" one. The image of the bus has shaken my father, and he is thankful my mother chose not to watch it. Noting that no details will be released on the television, my father calls the hospital.

"Your daughter is back in surgery," he is told. "When she came out of the first operation, we think Haley had some movement in her toes. But there is no longer movement, so they are operating again, trying to find out why."

My mother looks around the airport lounge and sees people resting, reading the newspaper and sipping coffee. "How can lives go on so normally when ours are turned upside down?" she asks only herself. She thinks, "My daughter is alone with her pain and fear.

Hold on, Haley, I'm coming." It is, as my father repeats again and again, a nightmare.

Finally, they land in Chicago, and connect right away to South Bend, running through the airport with only minutes to make their connection.

The sun is up in the east, and my mother scans the Indiana sky-line, looking for the hospital, looking for me, her daughter.

When my parents land in South Bend, the storm has abated, but the wind is still blowing. There is a lot of snow on the ground. They are not dressed for this and start to shake. Is it the cold or the fear of what is coming? Sister Kathleen Beatty, my "dorm mother," and my roommate, Alisha, meet them at the gate. Three men step up and introduce themselves: Dick Rosenthal, Director of Athletics; Rex Rakow, Head of Security; and Bill Kirk, Assistant Vice President for Student Affairs. They offer little information, but Bill offers my dad his coat.

My parents have only been in South Bend a few minutes, yet they are able to see why Notre Dame is such a special place. They will quickly realize that if something this horrible has to happen, this is the kind of place you want to be. The Notre Dame family is a cocoon, and although my mother could not be here to warm me, there are others who are glad to step in and do anything they can for one of their own. And I am one of their own. When my parents left me at school in August, they did not know that they too were a part of the Notre Dame family. But, as they stepped off that plane, the Notre Dame family became tangible, real and forever. Notre Dame is giving everything it has to us, and to everyone involved in the accident. And that is good, because we will need it all.

Mom and Dad see a familiar face when they arrive at the hospital: Nancy Martin, my best friend since childhood. On the surface, Nancy and I are opposites: she is blonde and outgoing, I am neither. I am athletic, she is not. But differences fade in a time of crisis, and my mom now sees this young adult who she remembers as a child going down the slide in our backyard pool. Nancy has taken over the role of directing phone traffic in the hospital waiting room, pro-viding updates and taking messages from my family members and friends who she has known for over ten years. She helps out the way a best friend does: behind the scenes and not looking for gratitude.

Dr. Keucher comes out to meet my parents.

He looks around at all the people and says, "Let's not talk here. Let's go to the chapel."

"This doesn't sound good," my mother whispers quietly.

The hospital chapel is tiny, no bigger than a small office. There is a loveseat on the side of the room, and Dr. Keucher leans against the wall, likely assuming my parents will sit. Mom does. Dad stands, which is perfect metaphor, for he likes to be on top of things to get a full view of difficult situations.

The doctor explains to my parents that I do not have feeling below my belly button and I am unable to move my legs. He tells them about my first surgery and that a recovery nurse thinks I did, at one point, move a toe. He states there are conflicting reports about whether I walked off the bus, but if I did, that is a good sign too. However, since shortly after the first surgery, he reports that I have had no movement at all. The second surgery revealed no clear signs of why I am paralyzed. Dr. Keucher says he did not find the blood clot he was hoping to find, which he would have removed in hopes of triggering the return of movement and feeling. As it stands, he tells them, the longer the paralysis lasts, the more likely it will be permanent. Right now, the focus is on a key 48-hour window. If movement is not back by Sunday, the prognosis will not be good.

My mother is speechless. She cannot think of any questions to ask.

My father suffers no such silence.

He shifts right into "attorney mode," as my mother calls it.

"What's her life expectancy now, will it be shortened?" my father asks.

"If she is in a wheelchair the rest of her life, then yes, that could shorten her lifespan some," Dr. Keucher answers.

"Will she have other complications?"

"Will she be able to have children?"

"How will her bladder function be affected?"

"Will she be able to control her bowels?"

My mom stares at my dad. She cannot believe the questions. But she also knows my father has his reasons for asking them. He is concerned about what the quality of my life is going to be.

Dr. Keucher maintains eye contact with my dad and answers what he can, basing his answers on the diagnosis of permanent paralysis.

Finally, my mother speaks and asks the only question that comes to her mind:

"Doctor Keucher, is there any hope?"

The doctor's face visibly drops as he looks at the ground. That in itself is an answer to my parents. After pausing, he whispers, "There is always hope."

Dr. Keucher is a neurosurgeon and not an orthopedic surgeon, the latter who specializes in reconstructing shattered spines. But my biggest obstacle is paralysis, directly related to my damaged nervous system, and a neurosurgeon is who I need. He knows to look for a blood clot or to check for a severed spinal cord. Additional specialists would be great, but in a small regional hospital, I am fortunate to have this doctor.

My parents go back to the waiting room. A nurse comes in, just as bouncy and perky as can be.

"Mr. and Mrs. Scott, did you see the doctor?" she asks.

"Yes," my mother responds. "I'm Haley's mom, Charlotte."

"Nice to meet you, I'm Shawn, Haley's recovery room nurse. Don't you worry, Haley is going to be fine," she says. "Dr. Keucher…well, you know, those doctors have to be careful what they say, because of all those personal injury lawyers."

My mom smiles.

"Nurse Shawn," my mother says. "I'd like you to meet my husband, Stephen Scott. He's a personal injury lawyer."

Everyone starts to laugh. My parents need this levity, need this smile; a reason to take the worry lines away for just a second, a moment to unclench their jaws. Then they are led to see me.

It is past noon, more than 12 hours after the accident, and I am waking up from my second surgery. I have not heard about any of the other girls' injuries, and I am hoping that no one else is in the hospital or seriously hurt. I get the best medicine I can hope for when I open my eyes and see my mother standing next to me.

"Hi, Mom," I say. "Where's Dad?"

My father had walked around the bed before I opened my eyes, and she points to him. Seeing my parents raises my spirits. Now that they are here, I know everything is all right. Parents are supposed to have that affect on their children, and my parents are definitely the best kind of parents. But the look on their faces concerns me. I do not want them to worry.

"It's okay, Mom," I assure her. "I still have my mind. I can still be a teacher."

My parents must have talked to someone on the way in and heard the news: Their oldest daughter, the tall, strong swimmer who had the world at her feet, could be facing the rest of her life in a wheelchair. I know my mother wants to cry, but I will not let her any more than she will let herself. Because I know that whatever news has them so down just is not true. Besides, looking at me, they can see I really am fine: I have no black eyes, no bruises, no broken arms or legs. I cannot feel anything in my legs or feet, and my back is a road map of incisions, stitches and bruises. But I am going to be fine.

I just have to be fine.

I will be…right?

4

We have always had a very close family. I was a typical "middle child," fiercely independent. I have an older brother, Stephen Jr., and a little sister, Mary Frances.

I was 10 years old when I started swimming competitively. Living in Arizona, where the sport is popular for several reasons, mainly the climate, I had swum my whole life, or had at least been in pools my whole life.

I improved as a swimmer as time passed. At just 10 years old, I was already 5-feet-8- inches tall. When I went to the pediatrician for a physical that year, my doctor told me I would be about 6-foot-2 fully grown. That was not good news to a pre-teen girl who already considered herself to be "freakishly tall." On the way out of the doctor's office, I told my mom, "I will not grow another inch." And I never did.

Being so tall for my age, I was a sprinter by physics. I would dive into the pool and already be ahead of everyone else just because of my height advantage.

There could be no doubt that swimming was "my sport." I had played several others: T-ball, soccer, dance, but none really worked out. I did show some promise at softball, so much in fact that I played baseball with the boys. I remember a "hardball" game where I hit a line drive to the outfield, but tripped while running to first base. My mother remembers telling my father, "It's okay, she's smart. She doesn't have to be an athlete." I was all arms and legs, and not very coordinated. I just could not, at that age, figure out how to use my body.

I eventually started swimming at our local country club in middle school, and then for my high school team and the local USA Swimming club.

Some of my friends were involved in sports. Other girls I knew became cheerleaders. But that wasn't for me; I did not have that bubbly personality, and while I had a few good friends, I was not a very social child.

High school classes were not very difficult for me. I took all the honors classes Xavier College Preparatory offered at the time and graduated with a 3.8 grade-point average. Because I was not very studious and found reading difficult, most of my knowledge came from class lectures. So even though my report cards indicated I was a good student, I really was not much of a student at all. I managed to get by with "A's" by paying attention in class and completing the required assignments.

During my junior year at Xavier, I had my first physical setback. It was a "typical swimmer" injury, born out of overuse of the rotator cuff, and it prevented me from swimming for six months. After physical therapy each day, I would still go to the pool but just to kick. This injury taught me valuable lessons: that I loved swimming and the rush of competition, and that I loved training hard and the challenge of a beatable opponent. As my rotator cuff healed, I was anxious to get back to full speed and compete again. In swimming's absence, I learned that I thrived on rising to the occasion and beating expectations.

I always knew that I would swim in college. It was more of a "where" I would swim rather than "if." I considered Michigan, Brown, Rice, Virginia, and the College of William & Mary. Notre Dame was not initially on my list of potential colleges.

Sister Lynn Winsor, Xavier's athletic director, changed that. A legend in Arizona high school sports, Sister Lynn has won more state championships as Xavier's golf coach than any other high school girls' golf coach in the United States. She works tirelessly and in every way is unforgettable. When Sister Lynn asked me where I was thinking of going to college, I told her my short list of schools.

"What about Notre Dame?" she asked.

Not being a Catholic, I had never thought about Notre Dame. I just shrugged my shoulders.

"You'd be perfect for them," she said. "Let me call the coach."

That afternoon she called Notre Dame Head Swimming Coach Tim Welsh. Coach Tim called me that night, and we set up a recruiting visit.

My recruiting trip could not have been scripted better. The description of Notre Dame's campus as this majestic, historical, and magical place did not begin to do it justice. The campus was so much more. The buildings were amazing architecturally, and the way the campus was designed was just breathtaking. More noticeably, and more importantly, the people were friendly—all of them. I was so surprised by how many people greeted me that day as I walked around campus. It was as if I had on a sign that read, "Be nice to me, I'm a recruit." Nancy went with me to visit her brother, who was a student at Notre Dame. Nancy toured and would end up going to St. Mary's College across the road.

My only concern with Notre Dame was the cold weather. I love a lot of things about Phoenix, but I particularly love the warm weather. However, the weekend of my recruiting trip in the middle of February, it was 60 degrees and sunny. All of the stories I had heard about cold, frigid temperatures were invalidated on that trip. I thought the 60-degree day was the norm, not the exception.

The trip, though, was not without its memorable events, most notably a dance at the Swim House. Susan "Scully" Bohdan, who would quickly become a confidante and life-long friend, was a sophomore the semester of my recruiting trip. She chaperoned me around, answered my questions, and made me feel like I belonged there.

That evening at the Swim House, people were mingling and having a good time, and once again I was struck by how friendly everyone was. I met one of the senior swimmers, Tracie O'Connell. She would graduate before I enrolled that fall, but she told me that night how she had "monogrammed" all four years. To her, and to me, that was a big deal, because not many people "letter" all four years in a varsity sport, at a major university. I added that to my list of goals. Enjoying myself but not really paying much attention, a guy turned around as he danced, swung his elbow and accidently hit me in the cheekbone, cracking the bone under my eye socket.

The next morning Scully took me to have breakfast with Coach Welsh. I was in a fog at that point, tired and with my face throbbing. I had not slept much because of the pain. Afterwards, Tim drove me to the airport. He seemed like a really cool guy in his trademark cowboy hat. I remember thinking he was pretty hip because he often used the word "cool." But again, it was his sincerity and kind demeanor that made me want to swim for him.

I flew first to Chicago and called my parents from the O'Hare Airport. I was not sure I could get back on another plane to fly to Phoenix. The air pressure made the eye pain more intense. Nancy held an ice pack on my face the entire flight from Chicago to Phoenix, as I laid in agony across three seats in the back of the plane.

Apparently the next day, Scully went into the swim coaches' office and told Coach Welsh about the incident, "I've got to tell you, Tim. There is no way Haley Scott is coming to school here."

However, as soon as I got off the plane, my parents asked how it went. I responded, "That's where I'm going to school." My cheekbone turned out to be fractured, but it was certainly nothing to override the great time I had, and the great people I met on the trip. There was no doubt that I would go to Notre Dame.

Coach Welsh offered, and I accepted, a partial scholarship. At the time, the swim program had only a few full scholarships to divide among more than a dozen swimmers. Plans were set for me to start that fall of 1991 at Notre Dame and to swim for the Fighting Irish.

Though I loved Phoenix, I was ready for something different. When the end of the summer rolled around, I was thrilled to be headed to Notre Dame. We packed boxes full of everything I would need for the dorm, including shampoo and soap, and shipped those ahead. I have no idea why we did not think they would sell shampoo in South Bend, but it was my first time leaving home.

As we flew to Chicago and drove to South Bend, I knew my mother would cry, and I gave her a hard time about it. So, of course, she did not cry. Once I got there I was more nervous than I thought I would be, but I was still ready for my parents and my younger sister to leave. I was at Notre Dame.

Notre Dame: In 1842, Reverend Edward Sorin, and seven other Brothers of the Congregation of Holy Cross founded the school on 524 acres known as St. Mary's of the Lakes. They changed the name of the land—granted to them with the understanding that they would build a learning institution—to reflect their native language:

L'Universite de Notre Dame du Lac. Constructing the buildings with clay drudged from the lakes, the University was officially chartered in January 1844. For the next 130 years, the University educated only male students. In 1972, then-President Father Theodore Hesburgh opened the school to women. To me, eventually.

I lived on the second floor in Lyons Hall with two other girls: Alisha and Theresa. Neither were swimmers, nor athletes for that matter. Notre Dame has a unique housing situation. Most students live on campus, and in the same dorm, all four years. The dorm takes on an identity, as do the students who live there. At a school without a Greek system, your dorm life becomes your social life. And when you are an athlete, you take on that team's identity and family closeness as well. My roommates and I shared two rooms, each about twelve feet by eight feet. It was pretty cramped.

But it was Notre Dame. So to me, it was all amazing and new, and I could not wait to meet my teammates.

5

Meghan Beeler lived in South Bend. One of her long-time friends was another swimmer in our freshman class, Angie Roby.

"We met when we were 11 or 12, maybe even earlier than that," Angie recalled. "Swimming is something you start at a young age, and it's something you do forever. In each state, you are at swim meets every weekend and you see the same people and they become your friends."

Meghan and Angie were such good friends that when the time came to pick a college, they took a pair of recruiting visits together.

"We went to Notre Dame at the same time on a recruiting trip and we went to a college in Nebraska on a recruiting trip," Angie said. "We both had a horrible time in Nebraska, and we were so happy that we were together because that was the only way we got through the recruiting weekend."

Meghan, as I said earlier, had a lot of qualities I admired. Angie saw those qualities as well as anyone. Meghan was a person with many interests and a lot of aspects to her personality.

"I saw all these different sides of Meghan," Angie said. "She was very carefree and always the spontaneous person, always fun and energetic. But then at Notre Dame, we were both business majors, so we had classes together as well. She was very serious when it came to classroom work, which was so weird for me, because I thought that she didn't care about that; but she really did, and was a great student."

Meghan's perfect 4.0 grade-point average her first semester was a great accomplishment for any college student, but especially for a student-athlete at a school with a rigorous academic program like Notre Dame's.

Meghan, as usual, was in top form after the Northwestern meet. She was "being her vibrant self," as Angie described it. Meghan was dating a senior on the football team, and he had given her a rose before we left for Northwestern.

"She walked to the locker room with that confident walk that she had," Angie said. "Lorrei and I laughed, because it was so Meghan. She had so much going for her. She was attractive, athletic, guys really liked her and she was smart."

In the locker room at Rolfs Aquatic Center, Amy Bethem's locker was right next to Colleen Hipp's. With the daily, close proximity they shared a lot of things. Colleen made a cassette tape of some music for Amy before the Northwestern trip. Amy had a ring of Colleen's. Colleen had borrowed Amy's shampoo to take on the trip. It was a familiar give-and-take relationship between swimmers, or any athletes.

"Colleen never had any drama in her life like a lot of us did, especially when it came to the frivolous things," Amy said. "She just really had her stuff together. She was not the kind to go out to parties, or into the social scene as much, but she was very kind and sweet."

In addition to being a student-athlete, Colleen was also in the Reserve Officers' Training Corps (ROTC) program, which required additional dedication and focus. She was exceedingly mature for a girl her age.

Scully, Lorrei, Meghan, Colleen, Amy, Angie. We were all getting to know our teammates, one by one. Friendships were formed and memories were being made.

Christmas Break at the end of the fall semester meant it was time for me to go home for the holidays. While I enjoyed Christmas with my family in Arizona, I missed the swim team. That January, Notre Dame played the University of Florida in the Sugar Bowl. My brother had graduated from Florida, so he had some fun ribbing me about how Notre Dame always got a better bowl bid than it deserved because of its reputation and tradition. My brother loved to repeat a joke from a popular campus shirt, "What's the difference between Notre Dame and Cheerios? Cheerios BELONGS in a bowl." We watched the game together at home, and much to my joy and my brother's chagrin, Notre Dame beat Florida.

I headed to Texas on January 3, 1992, for the winter training camp Tim Welsh had set up in Austin. For two weeks we lived and swam side by side, enduring Tim's famous "2400 (meters) for time," a grueling training set that lasted about 30 minutes. The training trip really brought the team closer together, especially the freshman class; we enjoyed the traditional "Freshmen Night Out," where our class spent the evening going out to dinner and socializing. I had been anxious to get back in the pool, and after camp, to get back to Notre Dame.

On Wednesday, January 22, the day before our road trip to Northwestern, we had the annual swim team Freshman Spaghetti Dinner, where the freshman class made dinner for the entire team. It was held at the clubhouse of the apartment complex where Randy, our assistant coach, lived. We used large kettles for pasta and one of the guys made a delicious spaghetti sauce. Lorrei, Colleen and I made dessert, "Dirt Cake," a recipe from Colleen's mother. It consisted of crumbled brownies, chocolate cake, crushed Oreos, and gummy worms, all in a flower pot. It "made the hair on the back of your neck stand straight up," in Randy's opinion. He also laughingly called it "death by chocolate."

Besides dinner, the highlight of the evening was skits by the freshman class. Beware the swimmer who had a random date, or other mishap, for it would be reenacted and revisited by the freshmen for the entire team's enjoyment. It was one more way in which the team bonded.

6

The trip to Northwestern the next day was routine for the seniors, as one of our captains, Shana Stephens, recalled:

"On the way to the meet we ate at the Old Country Buffet, which is kind of a wonderful place and horrible place at the same time," Shana explained laughingly. "There are just masses of food. They had one of those frozen yogurt bars and we all had just heaping portions of frozen yogurt with chocolate sprinkles and hot fudge and whipped cream. It is also a gross place because who knows how long the all-you-can-eat food has been sitting there.

"After the meet, in the locker room, our team was very wound up. We had swum well as a team, and we were getting better. More important on a personal level, we were becoming closer, with each class forming a unique bond.

"We laughed and danced, and people stood up on the locker room's wobbly benches, still in their towels after showering, and sang goofy songs," Shana said. "There are a couple of songs I remember: 'OPP,' MC Hammer, and a (dance mix) remake of 'Oh What a Night' (by Frankie Valli and the Four Seasons). Meghan in particular always sang that 'OPP' song. We had a boom box and we would play those same songs over and over," Shana remembered.

"The atmosphere was really warm, friendly and fun, even though we got beat by Northwestern. I think we were thrilled that we had been able to compete with a higher caliber team."

Shana sat near the back of the bus, in the seat directly in front of Colleen. Meghan was one of the last swimmers to return to the bus. She was still in a great mood from the meet.

"In the aisle of the bus after we got on the road, Meghan stood up and did a dance; she was just a riot," Shana remembered. "I think it was 'OPP,' (performed by Naughty by Nature). This was the beginning of the trip home, right before the movie started. Then the exhilaration wore off a bit and people were settling in and studying.

It is not a real long bus ride by any means, so it wasn't like people were sleeping, per se, because the trip is only a little more than two hours."

Coach Tim Welsh sat up front in his usual seat just behind Howard, our usual driver.

"The women watched a movie. It was not a movie I wanted to watch," Tim said. "So I was looking at the season at that point. We had scheduled a women's meet on Thursday, a men's meet on Friday, and a combined meet on Saturday. So I was looking at tomorrow's meet. For most of the way back, they were watching the movie and I was working on the next day's meet."

Tim remembered when the snow started to fall more noticeably about an hour from home, and then near the city of LaPorte, Indiana, it started snowing badly.

"At that point obviously I stopped working and just watched the road," Tim recalled. "There was also a point where there was a long way between exits. My recollection is that during the worst part of the snow storm we were in that long stretch, where we had passed the last exit to get off the Toll Road and the next exit was the South Bend Airport exit. When we got to that exit, the snow lightened up, and I remember saying to Howard, 'It was pretty bad back there,' and Howard nodded in agreement. We weren't even five miles from campus at that point, and in our minds we had come through the worst part of the storm."

Shana studied for a while, before another senior, Cyndi Safford, asked her to come up front to help her with her Spanish homework.

"We did that while watching the end of the movie," Shana said. "All the lights were off, except the reading lights. We huddled together on the left side, the driver's side of the bus, a seat or two behind Amy Bethem and Angie Roby.

"I vividly remember I had taken off my boots and was sitting cross-legged," Shana said. "That became one of my quirks after the accident; I now never take my shoes off in an airplane or a bus, because I remember walking around barefoot in the snow afterward."

While most of us noticed the weather, Shana did not.

"One interesting point is I had no perception of the weather. I did not know we were in a snowstorm. I was in this warm little place traveling down the highway, watching a sad movie and studying with a friend," Shana said.

Tim remembered some movement, particularly in the front of the bus as people put shoes back on, and gathered their books and other belongings.

"I put my shoes on, closed up the stuff I was working on, and reached for my coat," Tim said.

He reached, but never quite got it.

"We moved into the passing lane and passed a car, and when we attempted to come back into the right lane, that is when the bus started to swerve about 90 degrees, and we kept going," Tim said. "I could not have told you this at the time, but that is what initiated the accident, as I now understand it. I heard Howard say, 'Okay, here we go,' to warn us to brace ourselves, and when we got into the bottom of the gully the bus flipped. I remember two loud noises, two different hits; one when the bus hit whatever made us flip, and then another."

Shana was still helping Cyndi with her Spanish when the bus began to slide.

"We were doing homework when the movie ended, and I remember thinking, 'Oh, jeeze, that was awfully sad. Did we really need to watch that movie?'" Shana said. "I think the credits were either just ending or had just recently ended, and that is when I remembered seeing Tim, at the front of the bus, turn around. My memory sees him in slow motion saying, 'Hold On!' in a loud and panicky voice."

As the bus started to slide, the back flipped around like a dog chasing its tail.

"There was a swerving motion, and something that I later identified as a very distinct lack of control: You are in a universe and something is happening to you, around you. That kind of feeling," Shana said. "But I remember the swerving, and then the crash sounds; at least one very loud crash, maybe two: a hit and then a flip. I do not know if that is accurate with the physics of the accident. But I remember the loud noise and then darkness, and then coldness.

"I don't know why, but I had a real sense of peace during the actual, physical, part of the accident," Shana continued. "I was completely absent from a sense of fear or panic or danger. I sat there, with snow already blowing in from the opening next to me, where one of the windows had come out."

Angie Roby, as she always did, sat in a window seat next to Amy Bethem, near the front of the bus on the driver's side.

"I remember spinning, and seeing this big ravine, and there were trees on the other side, and I kept thinking, 'Please don't let me die, please don't let me die.' We just hit something that caused us to kind of go onto our side. It was all one continuous motion," Angie recalled. "But when we were sliding around—and this is one thing that bothered me with the police—at the time they said that the windows never popped out. But they did. The windows popped out, because that was one of the things that was so vivid in my mind as we were spinning; it was like suction, and the windows just…burst out. I remember thinking, 'Oh my God, don't let me fly out this window.' The window popped out but it did not break. It wasn't that the bus went on its side and the window shattered; it just popped out."

Later, investigators determined that the varying speeds and directions of the bus created a lot of torque, which probably triggered a release mechanism on the windows.

"At one point, I ended up with one arm stuck outside the bus, where the window had been," Angie said. "The whole thing only took a couple of seconds, but it felt like we slid forever. I kept thinking that we would keep going and hit the trees. It was like being on a tilt-a-whirl ride, with the whipping propulsion from the back."

Angie also had one of her legs caught in a seat, and one leg dangling down.

"Tim came over to me, and I was stuck, spread eagle," Angie said. "I kept saying 'Please don't leave, please don't leave.' I was just so freaked out. Everyone was telling me, 'Don't move' because they did not know if I was hurt, if I had broken a limb, or worse. I remember being freezing, just shaking uncontrollably. People started to come to the scene pretty quickly, though I remember at the time thinking it didn't seem that quick. But I had to move, I had to get out. I tried to pull my arm free. I couldn't lay there another second."

Tim was thrown forward and to the passenger side.

"When the bus came to rest, I was on my back in the stairwell where you enter and exit the bus," Tim said. "So I was thrown out of my seat and I wound up on my back part way down those stairs. There were all kinds of commotion obviously at that time. Howard, the bus driver, was already on the phone reporting the accident. I remember moving back toward where my seat was, and there were a couple of girls there. One of those girls—I can't remember who, Angie Roby or another—was having trouble getting her arm out from under the seat. I remember staying with her until she was able to wiggle free, and then we climbed through the front windshield."

As the bus flipped and came to a rest the team collided with the ceiling, looking upward at the seats in which they had sat a moment earlier.

Angie turned and saw a teammate.

"I remember seeing Angela Gugle and noticing her face. She was cut and her face was covered in blood," Angie said. "I think I saw Shana Stephens next, one of our senior captains, and she and a couple of others were literally trying to lift the bus; they had their hands where the windows would have been, and it seemed like they were trying to lift the bus."

When light finally illuminated the cabin a bit, or perhaps as her eyes adjusted to the dark; Shana looked around and, as Angie did, saw Angela.

"One of the divers, Angela Gugle, had a lot of blood on her facing, dripping into her eyes. She was right in front of me, screaming, 'I can't see! I can't see!' I could tell that all the blood came from a gash on her forehead, so I found something, wiped it away, and told her, 'Angela you are fine, you can see; it's just blood in your eyes, and you are going to be fine.' She and I helped each other out of the bus. That is when I first recall realizing how serious the situation was, and I felt my perception sway."

Scully, who had been sitting next to me, immediately got off the bus and was somewhat disoriented.

"Have you ever seen movies where an accident happens and the vehicle explodes? That is what I had in my head," Scully said. "So my first instinct was to get out. I was, by far, the first one off the bus. Thankfully I was able to move.

"Basically the way the bus was situated, you had to go down a little bit into a ditch and then run up a hill. So that is what I did," Scully said. "I started running toward South Bend. I was just running, running, running...then I looked back and thought, 'Oh my God, am I the only one who survived?' That was my original thought because I was alone, outside, off the bus and running. Then I saw people moving slowly, and I thought, 'Okay, I am still alive, so I'd better go back.' That's when I saw Haley."

After the accident when I got off the bus, Scully claimed I walked three steps and fell on the fourth. I fell into a foot of snow. The next thing I remember was Scully sitting next to me and Lorrei standing over me, just staring. I mostly remember feeling Scully's presence next to me, but I can still see the lost, blank look on Lorrei's face. Lorrei was knocked senseless and suffered a concussion in the accident.

The windows in front of and behind her popped out causing Meghan (sitting behind her) and Colleen (seated directly in front of her) to be thrown out of the bus as it flipped upside-down. Lorrei's life was saved when her head slammed into the metal divider that separated those two windows. No one celebrates a concussion, but that night it saved Lorrei's life. I watched Lorrei walk away speechless, not understanding her lack of words.

Scully stayed with me. Her training as a lifeguard prepared her for injury, though probably not of this cause, and she was not about to let someone with a potential spinal injury be moved. That was when I asked her to remove my gum.

"That's when I knew Haley was hurt," Scully said. "I laughed when she said it, not that there was anything funny about what was going on, but if Haley did not want her gum, she really was hurt."

Just as Scully helped me, other teammates helped one another.

"When I got out of the bus, one of the first things that struck me was how calm people were and how attentive they were to helping one another," Tim said. "There was not any hysterical screaming. There was a lot of, 'Let's go here. Let's move over there. Have you seen somebody? Take care of yourself.' There was a lot of good, calm, on-site help. There were already cars that had stopped and people who were coming down to help out. I remember walking around the bus a little bit and then I met up with Shana Stephens. She and I then walked around the bus together, to each of the groups, intentionally looking for everybody. We tried to take attendance.

"I remember seeing Haley lying on her back, packed in snow," Tim said. "I can remember Scully's calming voice. I could not tell you where Scully was standing or sitting, but I remember hearing her voice."

He and Shana continued to walk around the accident site, with a roster, trying to find everyone.

"We could not account for three people," Tim said. "One of them was Meghan, one of them was Colleen, and another freshman Michelle Lower.

"It was almost two hours later, before we left the hospital that I finally saw Michelle and I said, 'Whew,' and gave her a hug."

No one knew that Michelle had been picked up by a truck driver who had taken her to the hospital; a great act by a Good Samaritan, but one that contributed to the fears that perhaps another swimmer was under the bus, because no one had seen her leave.

Not everyone was able to get out of the bus right away.

"Someone was pinned," Shana said. "Many of the girls were still in the bus as I helped Angela out, and then I went back in and was helping people, just taking their arm and helping lead them out. It was pretty awful."

Shana said Angela was also disoriented.

"I think she was completely in shock, because at that time she was being very polite, 'Excuse me, can you help me out?' That's when the whole scenario became pretty surreal," Shana said. "I think that my experience is different from a lot of people's because I was not physically injured in the least. People were crawling out and crying, and a lot of people were in a lot of physical pain. Kristin Heath broke her collarbone. Michelle Lower and one of our divers had lacerations."

Shana saw a pair of pink goggles among the accident's clutter.

"Meghan had a pair of wild pink goggles, which everyone on the team really liked," Shana said. "Several of the other girls had picked up the same set of goggles. We had worn them for a couple of weeks, but I remember at that meet in particular it was kind of a bonding thing. I remember feelings of unity, friendship and cohesiveness.

"One thing that was kind of powerful for me, after the accident Notre Dame security had gathered all of our things that had been scattered about the accident site, and we all picked through to take our stuff back," Shana said. "Looking through the bin, I found a pair of pink goggles. To me that was such a sign of Meghan's fun and youthful spirit. So I asked her parents if I could have them afterwards, and they said I could, so I have kept those for a long time."

Diane Walton and Julie Schick, both freshmen, had been sitting in the back row next to Meghan.

"I can picture Diane and Julie, they were in the back of the bus near the lavatory, and they were covered in that blue stuff (from the commode)," Shana said. "That was one of those really funny-horrific kinds of things. They are both blond, and I remember saying, 'You dyed your hair' just to be loving and supportive. Their hands were very cut up and would require multiple corrective surgeries. Both were terrified, so I held their hands and told them both, 'You are going to be okay, let's get you outside. And by the way, your hair is blue and it looks lovely.' I was trying to be funny in a nurturing way.

"Once we got a group of people—some with blood and torn clothing—off the bus, we formed a circle, holding arms, and said the 'Our Father.' We really leaned on our faith at the time and I recalled something my mom had recently said to me, 'If God leads you to it, He'll help you through it.'"

Angie saw her good friend Lorrei walking around.

"I remember I was like, 'Lorrei, oh my God!' and she was just in a daze, very confused, more than just being in shock," Angie said.

The truck drivers who stopped could not have been more generous or caring. Angie and Amy, and two other swimmers, were taken by one truck driver into the cab of his 18-wheeler.

"We just sat there and said the 'Hail Mary' over and over again," Angie said. "We did that until someone came to get us."

Still, it caused more disorganization in terms of having more people in the mix and trying to account for all the swimmers.

"The truckers started to come, and there was kind of a mixed feeling. You know, these strangers were taking some of the girls into the back of their trucks," Shana said. "And I remember Tim and I were a little confused like, 'What is going on?' and there was a little bit of chaos around that scene. These people, these men, were very helpful and very supportive, but it was nonetheless odd."

The bus driver, Howard, had called for another bus immediately after the crash, and that bus showed up within a half an hour.

"Several of the swimmers were taken in an ambulance," Shana said. "I think Haley for sure was taken in an ambulance right away, and maybe there were others who went early as well, but most of the people got on the bus (which Howard called), and then we were trying to get everybody out of the truckers' cabs, and onto that bus."

The search for the missing swimmers intensified, and this second bus was used as a makeshift "triage" center.

"People had started crying, and wounds were being tended to on the triage bus. Coach and I grabbed a Notre Dame swim bag, and I found a roster inside, so we went through it and started checking off names. But what we were doing was a head count; counting our friends and colleagues. Coach and I had a pact that we would not check anybody off the list until we looked them in the eye. If someone said 'I saw so-and-so in a truck cab,' we would go to the truck cab and look them in the eye. And it was at that point that we found Colleen."

Assistant Coach Randy also saw Colleen. Trapped underneath what is believed to be a metal support or possibly a window partition, was the lifeless body of our sweet, kind teammate.

"It was horrible," Shana said. "When I talked to her family afterwards, I could only say that I really felt it was peaceful, in a really sad way."

Trooper Kevin Kubsch, of the Indiana State Police, was working that night, even though it was not his normal shift. He had been called into work earlier in the afternoon when the storm hit.

"Normally I work midnights," Kubsch said. "We had been called out earlier because of the snow storm, and we had some white out conditions in the area where the bus traveled. There were a lot of accidents and vehicles that had gone off the roadway."

Trooper Kubsch's brother, who was a county deputy, was riding with him that night. Around midnight, they had taken a break with two other county deputies at a Shoney's restaurant located right off the Notre Dame/South Bend exit.

"It was the first chance we had to sit down and get a cup of coffee or something to eat," Kevin Kubsch said.

The call came over Trooper Kubsch's radio that a bus had gone off the roadway on the Toll Road, and was down in the ditch. Kubsch and his brother got into their car, and the two deputies got into another, and headed that way. As they went past the tollbooth, traffic was barely moving in the whiteout conditions.

"It was really slow going," Kubsch said. "The weather was horrific. The wind was blowing hard and the snow was blowing. At the time you couldn't travel more than 45 miles per hour on the Toll Road; that's how difficult it was that night. The radio dispatcher called us again and said they believed this was a roll over and there were possible injuries involved."

Going the opposite direction on the Toll Road to get to the location, Kubsch had to pass the accident site from the other side of the road.

"You couldn't cross over in the median, so I had to turn around, and I slid past the darn cross over. It was so slick in the passing lanes," Kubsch said. "But we got turned around.

"I saw three or four truck drivers that had stopped and were trying to lend assistance. It was incredible how those guys were trying to provide for the gals."

Once on the scene, Trooper Kubsch started running down the hill and saw the wreckage and chaos.

"I'll never forget this: When I started running down the hill, I found part of this window that had apparently broke free and was lying in the snow. You couldn't tell it was a window because it was white, all covered in snow," he said. "I hit that thing and fell right on my back. I went right down the embankment, which was pretty steep."

The bus was "actually facing the opposite way it was going, and I could see the undercarriage of the vehicle."

He saw one swimmer pinned to the ground by the metal partition separating the windows, likely the very partition that saved

Lorrei's life when she hit her head on it and kept her from falling out as the bus flipped.

Kubsch looked at one of the truck drivers and started to ask, "Is there any way…"

"No, there is nothing anyone can do," the truck driver interjected.

At that point Kubsch went back up the hill and saw several Notre Dame swim parkas scattered in the snow.

"Until then I had no idea that it was a charter bus for Notre Dame. I didn't want to see a whole lot of media. So instead of calling it in on the radio, I called the rest of the information in on my cell phone. Then I called an assistant athletic director at Notre Dame, who I knew always worked on Thursday nights."

Kubsch left his vehicle and again approached the crash. The second time heading down the embankment, Trooper Kubsch stepped to avoid the window, but hit a hole completely covered with snow and stumbled again. It was that kind of night. He was in "first responder mode," assessing injuries, and thinking only of what needed to be done for others. He is that type of man.

"I noticed a young lady on her side, on the embankment, near the top of bus—I later found out that she was Haley Scott—and there was another student kneeling with her," Kubsch said. "I walked up and started speaking with the other girl, Scully. Haley was on her side, and if there was a spinal cord injury, that was not the place for her to be. I told Scully, 'We have to stabilize her.' So I gave Scully a quick course on how we were going to move Haley onto her back. I said, 'I want you to hold her head, and I will count to three, then we will roll her over onto her back.' We did, and we covered her up to try and keep her warm. Then I told her to keep holding Haley's head and keep talking to her while I ran to get the paramedics."

The first paramedic on the scene was a "young man I've known for years," Kubsch said. "I told him, 'I think we have two deceased, but until we can get a wrecker up here, there's nothing we can do for them.' The rest of the girls were pretty much walking wounded."

Kubsch directed the paramedic to me.

"I believe this young lady is the most serious for your triage," Kubsch said.

7

Friday Evening.

My parents are asked if they wish to attend Mass at the Basilica, but they decline. They have just gotten here and cannot leave me. I am wheeled into the Intensive Care Unit with my parents by my side.

My mother is surprised by the ICU. Her knowledge is that it can be cold, threatening and frightening, but she thinks, "This room isn't that." My room is well lit, and I have all kinds of balloons and flowers already. There is a teddy bear in a hammock.

"What a good place to be under the circumstances," my mother thinks. "This will be okay for now."

My father tells my mother and me that my brother is on a plane and scheduled to arrive this evening. He is coming from Atlanta, where he is just starting a new job. My mother wrestles with this: She cannot take care of another child. She already has her hands, and emotions, more than full enough with me.

The nurse on duty pricks my toes, feet and legs with a pin, but I have no feeling, no pain. Even my abdomen produces no sensations when she pokes me there. I know this is not good, but no one says anything to that effect.

When my brother arrives, the dynamics of our family change. At a time when we most need it and least expect it, the boy my parents raised is now a man, a mature adult who understands what his role is during this time of crisis. Stephen, tall and strong, walks right in, and his aura of confidence and humor makes me feel better immediately. He tells our mother, "Mom, go get something to eat."

At first, my mother resists.

"Stephen, I need to stay with Haley," she insists. "Because…"

"Mom, it's time for you to take a break," he says with a new found authority. "You need to take care of yourself too."

He helps her up by her arm, and announces that he will spend some "quality time" with me because I am a "captive, though who knows how attentive, audience," and "if she's lucky," he might even try out some new material. My brother has this amazing affect on me; he can always make me smile.

Even now.

Thank God, even now.

My brother quickly immerses himself in my world. He finds out which IV is giving me what, which tube functions in what role, who my doctors and nurses are, and what I think of them all. Then, because he is my older brother, Stephen playfully wonders aloud just how long I am "going to milk this thing for." I love my brother.

Then it is my turn.

"Hey, Stephen," I say. "Watch the heart monitor."

He looks, locates it, and looks back at me.

"Check this out," I say, closing my eyes. I let out a deep breath through my nose, and go to a place mentally where no one can find me.

The monitor pings along in the 80 to 90 heartbeat-per-minute range. In just a couple of minutes, I bring it down to 40 beats-per-minute.

"That," he says admiringly, "is so cool."

I open my eyes, and he is grinning, proud of his kid sister.

"How do you do that?" he asks.

This boy, who I now realize is a man, has amazed me my whole life. He is good-looking, funny, and a great dancer; he is the brother every little sister would love to have.

"You know how you can wiggle your ears?" I ask, and he nods. "Well, this is something I can do."

He starts laughing, and so do I. If I could run across the room and jump into my big brother's arms, I would.

And I will.

Just not yet.

The door opens and Dr. Klauer comes in. My brother is introduced to the man who, until Stephen arrived, was in charge of keeping my spirits high and my attitude positive. Dr. Klauer begins to coach me on focusing on the positive. I close my eyes, relax and listen to Dr. Klauer's calm voice. He asks me to think of something from my childhood: something strong, something alive. I recall a mulberry tree in my front yard, one that we used to climb when we were younger, that seemed large as a child, but got smaller as we grew up.

Dr. Klauer likes this. "A tree is good," he says, and continues slowly in his meditative voice. "Think of that mulberry tree. Think of its strong trunk, and think of your spine as the trunk of that tree. The trunk is strong. Your spine is strong; it is healing and getting stronger.

"Now, think of the branches on the tree. The branches are your nerves, the nerves that extend down your legs to your toes. The branches on the mulberry tree are strong, and so are the nerves that carry messages to your legs. Think of them as strong. Think of them as alive. Think of them as healing."

My eyes are closed and I am listening to Dr. Klauer's words. I take them to heart; I take them to my legs. I reach deep inside myself and focus on what he is saying. I have to. I do not have a choice. I think of the tree, of the trunk, of the branches and of my body. Be strong. Be alive. Heal. This goes on for several minutes.

"Haley," Dr. Klauer's voice brings me back to him. "Keep thinking these thoughts. Think of the tree, think of the branches. Think of your spine healing and strengthening. The more you practice sending messages to your legs, the better chance they have of finding a way to get there."

I need this training, and I honestly enjoy it. But my brother sees this mental imagery session in a different light. When I open my eyes, I see Stephen making mystical and wide-eyed faces behind Dr. Klauer, and I get the great feeling of laughter bubbles in my belly. Laughter, often a drug of sorts, is suddenly sustenance.

For the first time all day, I am not smiling for visitors, but I am forcing a smile away, keeping it from creasing my face. Dr. Klauer reminds me to continue with the imagery, and leaves the room. My brother dubs him "Yoda" and says, "May the force be with you." This brother, who can deadpan Eddie Murphy from the restaurant scene in *Beverly Hills Cop*, has now added *Star Wars* to his repertoire. I am so glad Stephen is here. I realize that this event that has landed me on my back has pulled the rug from under him, too. But I cannot feel badly for the disruption of his life, because Stephen won't let me. He just won't, because in the bag of tricks he brought with him, he has only faith and laughter.

Another visitor asks to see me and I am so glad she has come. It is Lorrei, who I have not seen since the accident site, when she walked away from me looking disoriented. She comes into my room wearing a neck brace. We are often mistaken for each other, but would not be tonight. She has on her long, navy blue wool coat, which she often wears, and her hair is blow-dried straight, which it often is.

Normally, the team would give her a hard time for this, because most of us do not mind messy "swimmer's hair"; but not Lorrei, who is usually the last one out of the locker room because she is busy blow-drying her hair. Tonight Lorrei looks different, and it is not just her neck brace. Perhaps she is wearing makeup, something those of us in our little group would never do unless it was a special occasion. I sincerely hope coming to see me does not qualify as a special occasion, even if I am in a hospital bed.

She looks sad and frightened, and I worry about her. Maybe she is hurt more than the doctors, or even she herself, realize.

"Hey, I'm going to be all right," I tell her. "Really, I am going to be fine."

This does nothing to ease her mind, and I cannot decipher what is going on in her head. Lorrei hardly says anything, which is not like our friendship. Times like this, I am quickly learning, it is hard to know what to say. The right words are almost impossible to find; sometimes silence and a careful hug are easier. She leaves the room, and leaves me concerned for her.

My mom returns, but I send her quickly back out.

"Mom," I say, as my mom leans closer, "something is wrong with Lorrei. Please go be a mom to her. Don't let her be alone and tell her I am going to be okay."

My mom disappears into the hallway to find Lorrei. What I do not know is that Lorrei's own mother is waiting for her right outside my room. My mom stops in the hallway to talk with Dr. Klauer and my father. I sense something is going on, but I do not know what.

More visitors, mostly teammates and other Notre Dame friends, fill the Intensive Care hallway. But they are turned away. It has been less than 24 hours since the accident, and I need to rest. They are told they may be able to visit me tomorrow.

My brother decides it will be his job to spend the nights with me and my parents can "do" the days. He shoos them off and sits down for a sibling chat. He tells me all about his girlfriend, Marcia, and I complain about my non-existent love life. I doze in and out depending on how often I press my PCA (patient controlled analgesia) pump. I love this button and the "ding" it makes, meaning the pain will soon fade.

While I rest, my brother flips through the channels on the television. He pauses on the local news, and I hear, "...two Notre Dame students killed..."

Stephen quickly changes the channel.

"Oh my God, my poor school!" I say to my brother, "first the bus accident, and then that? How can two bad things happen at Notre Dame in the same day?" In my fatigued, confused and pain-medicated state, the obvious is not so obvious.

Stephen diverts my attention by asking me to lower my heart rate again. I turn to look at the monitor, take a deep breath, relax and regain my calm focus. My brother, who my parents always felt dodged responsibility, is suddenly a pro at taking charge. He helps me avoid the horror and guides me to find my base of strength to sort through the scattered pieces of my young life.

"You need to focus on getting better. No swelling, no pain," he imitates Dr. Klauer and his smile lights up the room. Stephen is funny, and everyone knows it, especially him. "Come on, Luke, use the force. Listen to Yoda."

Saturday is a big day. I made plans through a teammate to get my mother a Notre Dame sweatshirt for today, her 45th birthday. She smiles as she slips it on, and she thanks me repeatedly, stunned that I remembered her birthday, given the circumstances. It was the least I could do. I can tell this is incredibly hard on her, but she's making this as close to bearable as it can be for me. I need her and she knows it, so she is here because she's a mom. Mine. She jokes with my father for forgetting, but my mother admits that even she herself had forgotten until I gave her the sweatshirt. She jokes with my brother that he too forgot. I consider pointing out that I remain their favorite child, as I have claimed since childhood. But then I realize, right now, my brother gets my vote for the favorite. He is stepping up in ways my mother never could have imagined. He is very much like my father in all the right ways, and yet he has a softer side very much like my Mom. She was right: She did not need to take care of another child. In her wildest dreams she could not imagine that this boy, who she took care of for so long, would be so good at taking care of her, and me, when we need it the most.

My feet, legs and abdomen are tested again with the pins. Despite the poking, I feel nothing. The nurse packs up the needle kit and quietly leaves my room. No one knows what to say or wants to say it.

The switch is made. Stephen leaves for a good day's rest and my parents begin their hospital routine. My father is tracking down all sorts of people to discuss various issues. He charts my progress here at Memorial Hospital and makes phone calls to make plans for what is next: what specialists I might see if further surgery is needed, or to what rehabilitation institutions I might be headed if I do not improve. He tirelessly works the phones to follow up on the advice and suggestions of family and friends while my mom mothers me. Dad has a yellow legal tablet to jot down questions as fast as they enter his mind, and then he asks the questions when it is appropriate. My father does not cry much, nor is he overly emotional; still I can see in his eyes that he is scared for me. We are so much alike and because of this, he is great company for me. Medication can only do so much.

But there is something else going on, something I do not know. I see it on my parents' faces when Dr. Klauer comes in the room. The three of them surround my bed. Dr. Klauer, on my right, leans close to my pillow with my dad standing next to him. My mom is on the other side of my bed.

I can tell by their eyes and their body postures that this is not good. My Intensive Care room, filled with the dull hum and beeps of machines, seems to be silent. I brace myself the best I can.

"Haley," Dr. Klauer says, "we have not lied to you about anything since the accident. You have asked if anyone else on the team was in the hospital, and we told you truthfully that no, you were the only one hurt enough to still be in the hospital. You are the only one who had surgery. But Haley, we did not tell you the entire truth. And now, it is time."

My mother puts her hands on my arm and moves closer to me on one side; and my father, holding my right hand tight in his, closes in on the other, as though they are trying to shield me from something bad, something hurtful, something that might bring more pain.

It is 10 a.m. on Saturday morning. My mother is wearing her new Notre Dame Swimming sweatshirt, and my father is looking at me with the love a father only has for his daughter. My mother's lips are pressed together as she blinks back tears that want to escape, but cannot. Not yet. Not in front of me.

"Meghan and Colleen died in the accident," Dr. Klauer tells me in a voice barely above a whisper. "They were thrown out of the bus window, and passed away instantly."

Tears well up in my eyes and I look to my mother. She gives me a reassuring look that says all at once: it's true, I am so sorry, but we will get through this.

I begin to cry. Mostly because I think I should. But really, I am in shock.

Key pieces of this unevenly sided puzzle start to fall into place. The two deaths reported on the television were my teammates, my classmates, my friends. Girls my age. Teens. College girls. Dead.

"Poor Lorrei," I think. Two of her closest friends are gone and a third friend is paralyzed. No wonder she looked so sad and scared last night. She had just returned from a Memorial Mass for Meghan and Colleen at the Basilica on campus, and she was afraid she might lose me as well.

Then the tears return. They are real and they do not stop. I turn to my mom and plead, "I have to walk for them. I will walk for them. And when I can swim, I will swim for them too."

My mom leans down to hug me. "I know you will. I know..." she says to comfort me and herself.

Then I have questions; questions about the Memorial Mass and the families.

I am told the Memorial service was beautiful. Celebrating life, especially at the time of death, is something Catholics do well. The service was videotaped, and I am told that whenever I am ready to watch it, I can.

My mother explains that Meghan's family is coming by later this morning to see me. Although they live in South Bend, I have never met them before. Last November, the Beelers had generously invited me to their house for Thanksgiving, but I had made other plans. I shared Thanksgiving dinner with the MacLeod family. John MacLeod, Notre Dame's new basketball coach, had coached my cousin in the NBA, and his nieces and nephew attended my mom's preschool. As much as I enjoyed the holiday with the MacLeod's, my focus now is on Meghan and her family, and I am sorry to have missed an opportunity to meet them prior to today.

I see Meghan's mother first and notice how much she looks like Meghan, down to the blue mascara that both Meghan and I liked to wear. She and her husband, whose eyes are glazed over with hurt and loss, have brought three of their younger children, who have lost their older, beautiful, popular, smart sister. More lives changed forever. I cannot imagine this family's pain. Despite my own predicament, I realize in this moment that I am fortunate and blessed to be alive.

Mrs. Beeler takes my hand and tells me that she has our *Three Amigos* picture at their house, and that Meghan had loved it. I feel helpless, and at the same loss for words that others feel when they visit me. With all they have lost, I can give them only what I have: a thin slice of hope and a promise that their daughter will not be forgotten.

"Meghan will always be with me," I say.

It is an honest sentiment. I do feel that Meghan and Colleen are with me right now, and I know they will be for a long time.

The Beelers leave to get ready to bury their daughter in two days; their daughter, their big sister, who they all adored. My classmate. My teammate. My friend. The girl I wanted to be like in many ways. And she is dead. I start to cry, and I feel heavy tears run down my cheeks.

My mother leaves my room with the Beeler family and watches them exit the ICU. My mother blots at tears she has cried for the mother she just met who has lost her daughter. In my mother's mind, life and its meaning have just crystallized: No parent should outlive their children. No matter what is ahead for us, there is worse, and she just saw it in Mrs. Beeler's face.

On her way back to my room, a kind-hearted visitor tells my mother, "I'm here to see Haley. And Mrs. Scott, I am so, so sorry…"

My mother, in what will become a new habit, raises her hand to stop the sympathy, because she now realizes she is not worthy of it.

"I have my daughter, no matter what we're living through," she tells this woman, who is caught off guard. "No matter what we face, she is still Haley. We haven't lost her."

My mother comes back into my room, the tears gone, and conviction in her voice.

"You will walk for Meghan and Colleen," my mother tells me confidently. "You will swim for them. They will help you do it. And you will do it for them."

My parents are not the kind to say something insincerely, or to say something just for the sake of saying it. I can tell from her tone, from her eyes and from her heart that my mother honestly believes this. And I believe her too.

We are all finding our place on this journey. My brother, of course, showed up with everything already organized in his mind. My father is doing what he does best: taking care of everything so that my mother and I do not have to worry. And now, my mother has seen a light and has emerged from a shadow of her own. She sees that I may have a lot of obstacles in my path, torrents of emotions to work through and a great amount of pain to overcome. But she now sees the blessing of life, and she quietly thanks God that He has allowed me to escape this nightmare with my life.

"Thank you, God," my mother whispers quietly, peacefully. "Thank you so much for my daughter."

The rest of the day is a string of visitors. I cannot see it, but they are lined up in the Intensive Care hallway, 15 or 20 people at any given time, waiting for their turn to spend just a few minutes with me. And if I need to rest, they wait. Swimmers, classmates, professors, administrators; many of them need to see me as much as I need to see them. They bring me smiles, encouraging words and gentle touches. My mom keeps a list of who comes, not to keep a score card, but to help her remember to thank them later on. She recognizes the importance of each visitor to me while acknowledging her own limited memory.

Never far from my mind, however, are Meghan and Colleen. When a freshman teammate comes in my room, our eyes meet and turn to tears. Sometimes no words are spoken; but there is a bond, a knowing, and a united strength that we will all draw upon when we need it, and give to it when we can.

Also never far from my mind are my feet. My toes, painted bright red as I always do before a swim meet, are propped up with a pillow to prevent "drop foot." Because I am not able to sit up, or even slightly incline, my toes are all I can see at this time. Between visitors and even sometimes when they are here, my eyes are glued to my red toes, telling them to move, willing them to move. I cannot get over how strange a sensation it is to see my feet and not be able to feel or move them. My constant attention to my toes is part confusion as to why they won't move, and part determination to make them move.

I become obsessed. "Think of your spine as the trunk of the tree," I hear Dr. Klauer say. "Think of it as strong, as healing. Send messages down the branches, down the nerves in your legs and feet. They are strong and healing." Dr. Klauer's voice keeps me focused as it repeats over and over in my head.

By Saturday night I am exhausted. Exhausted from the news I received that morning; exhausted from the accident and surgeries the day before; exhausted from the many visitors who lifted my spirits and exhausted from practicing Dr. Klauer's imagery. The effort exerted sending messages from my "trunk" to my "branches" takes more energy than I have.

It is Sunday. I am so ready for a better day.

Yesterday I was told two teammates had died. I know they are with me now. I can see their faces so alive, and yet I know their lives have ended. It is hard to comprehend.

I have not had my feet or legs "tested" today to see if I have regained any feeling or movement. This is a staple of our routine and I wonder why it has not been done.

My mother comes in, and though she won't complain, she has a migraine. The nurses are not as upbeat as they usually are either. Maybe it is because they are working on Sunday and they wish they had the day off. That is how I would feel too. It is a solemn mood all around.

Laura, my day nurse, shoos my parents out so she can give me a sponge bath and change the bandage on my incision. She gives me more than that. She is always so kind, but today she has a look on her face that I have not seen before.

"You need to accept this so you can start to move on," she tells me.

"Accept what?" I ask.

"The paralysis," she says in a kind but firm tone. "The 48-hour window the doctors gave you has passed. You have to come to terms with this."

I do not reply, nor do I make eye contact with her. I just stare at my red toes. She continues, perhaps because she does not think I am listening to, or hearing, what she says.

"You will never walk or swim again. Your life has changed forever. You have to be prepared for what you are facing. The faster you accept it, the faster you will be able to work with what you are able to do. You can have a full life, but it will never be the same."

I start to cry. I can feel tears running from the corners of my eyes into my hair. I am not sobbing. She is correct that I cannot move my feet, but she does not understand that this is just temporary.

Laura leaves and speaks to my mom who is waiting outside my door. My mother knows I have enough on my plate and that I cannot, and should not have to, digest this right now. Mostly, though, my mother does not believe I will be paralyzed.

"You should see her swim," my mother says to Laura. "You could throw her in the pool right now and if it weren't for her incision on her back, she would pull herself through the water with her arms. Do you know anything about swimmers? These kids have their legs tied together in practice and swim with their arms—for fun! That's what swimmers do. Do not tell her she won't swim again. Just you watch."

The nurse is as caught off guard by my mom's response as my mother was by the nurse's pronouncement about the passing of the 48-hour deadline.

A determined mother returns to my side.

"Laura told me what she said to you," my mother's voice is strong and sure. "She doesn't know you. You will swim again."

I nod, because it is all I have the energy and emotion left to do.

Laura is just doing her job, to prepare my mother and me for what is ahead of us. She is saying we have a lot of work to do, and the sooner we accept the things out of our control, we can focus on those within our control. Laura has been a wonderful nurse and is not trying to hurt us. She honestly believes it is best for us to accept the paralysis.

My mother, despite my tears and because she has the strength of 10 people in her slender body, is able to manage a smile.

"I cannot wait to see her face," my mother says to me, "when you walk out of here, and when you swim again."

My brother, my on-location stand-up comedy act, comes over and whispers in my ear.

"Forget about what they say," he says. "I'll be right back."

He refuses to believe that I am going to be paralyzed and has to excuse himself.

Stephen shakes his head as he leaves the room. In the hallway, he overhears some doctors talking and listens in because, well, because he is a "Scott," and any information is good information—if we have it, that is. But hearing what they say, he turns back towards my room, walking slowly. He is trying to accept what he heard the doctors say, about how his sister will never walk again. Never walk again. Never walk again.

"Forget them," he says to himself. "They don't know Haley; they don't know my sister."

But then something happens, something he could not have foreseen. Because another visitor, Trooper Kevin Kubsch, is headed in to see me, Stephen pauses and stops at the doorway of the ICU room next to mine. The door is open and curiosity overtakes him, so he looks in. A girl, either my age or very close to my age, is propped up halfway resting peacefully.

Her eyes are closed, and on a clipboard on the wall behind her, is a sign written in big block letters, "Two blinks mean yes, one blink means no."

In all likelihood, this girl will communicate for the rest of her life by blinking answers. She won't function from the waist down; she won't even function from the neck down. Stephen, who deeply believes in a higher power, realizes this is a message to him: His little sister is going to be all right. I am still Haley. I can talk and laugh and joke and use my arms. I do not have to blink answers. He is done feeling sorry for me, and done feeling sorry for himself. No matter how bad the prognosis is for his younger sister, next door the world has really come crashing down on some other special girl, someone else's special daughter, maybe even someone's younger sister.

State Trooper Kubsch has come to visit me, but also to see my parents. He tells my mother he just needs someone to talk to about the accident, and to express his feelings. My mother is touched.

"I've just," Trooper Kubsch starts, pushing back tears, "never been through anything like this in my life."

My mother hugs him.

"None of us have," she tells him.

He has a teddy bear for me. A stuffed animal they give to kids who are caught up in life-changing trauma: domestic violence, fires, the death of a parent. He tells my mother he wants me to have this teddy bear.

Notre Dame, which has been incredible through every moment of this process, sends members of its security team to join Trooper Kubsch to take my parents out to the crash site on Sunday afternoon. My parents had chosen to wait because they did not want to see the bus. A wrecker has taken it away, and my parents decide they are ready to see the site of the accident.

Snow still covers the ground, with debris from the inside of the bus stomped into it. Police tape surrounds the crash site as investigators are still trying to piece together exactly what went wrong, where lives came apart and two lives ended.

My mother finds some Big Red gum wrappers in the snow. She recognizes my favorite brand of gum and the unique way I fold my empty wrappers, and knows they are mine. Waves of emotions hit her, yet she holds it together as she holds on to my father. Dazed, they leave the site and ride to the State Trooper Station just a quarter mile down the Toll Road and listen to a tape of the 911 call.

When my parents come back in to see me, they are tired and shaken from the visit to the accident site.

"No," Stephen says, leading them outside my room. "Put on your happy faces, because I need to tell you a little story."

My parents look confused.

"Listen," Stephen whispers, glancing at the girl in the room next to mine. "It could be so much worse."

A small man, maybe 5 feet 4 inches, shows up in ICU with a Western Union telegram for me. My mom intercepts him at the nurses' station.

"I have a telegram for Haley," he says.

"I'm her mother. I'll be happy to give it to her."

"I'd really like to give it to Haley myself," he says.

I am with the nurse, so my mom thanks him and says she will take it.

"I have something else for her," says this old man with a scruffy face, wearing a tweed coat, driving hat and muffler.

"I am sorry, she is not receiving visitors," my mother explains.

"Okay, I understand," he says compassionately. "Will you give her this for me?" he asks, and then reaches out and embraces my mother with a big hug.

"I will," my mother says, pushing back tears, amazed at the love this community has for her little girl, shown through a man we have never before met.

My mother comes in and gives me a Western Union hug. We smile. I hope he knows he made a dark day a little bit brighter.

Although it is Super Bowl Sunday, there is nothing super about it. Next to swimming, I love football. But for the first time in as long as I can remember, I do not care about the game. I do not know who is playing, but it is a blowout. And it is just a game. To millions of fans it is everything on this day; but to me, today, it means nothing.

There are fewer visitors today. Most have paid their respects, and those who do come will never stop coming. The mood tonight is as dark as the room—only temporarily lit by a blinking light or rare laughter or the bell as I push the button on my morphine drip.

There are knowing and fearful glances that the clock is ticking, but I do not notice. To me, it is all about my feet. Meghan, Colleen and my feet. Those red toes. "Move, damn it!"

My brother sees my focus and reads my face. "May the Force be with you," he says. He knows just when I need to smile.

The long day that is Sunday finally ends.

Monday is even quieter.

The funerals for Meghan and Colleen are this afternoon. Meghan's funeral is here in South Bend. Colleen's is in her home-town, St. Louis. The girls on the team are allowed to choose which they will attend. This team, united in tragedy, will be split in two for the funerals. Lorrei, who was the closest to both girls, decries having to pick between her friends. I feel so badly for her and what she is going through.

My parents are offered a tour of the hospital's rehabilitation floor this morning. They are shocked. There are wheelchairs everywhere and not just standard issue wheelchairs. Some of the chairs have extensive padding and most are high-backed. Many are outfitted with straps to hold the person upright. There are lifts to move patients into specialized bathing tubs or into their beds. Most of the patients are old enough to be my grandparents.

"We can teach Haley to cook in a wheelchair," the woman explains to my mother in an upbeat voice. "She will even learn how to make her bed while in her chair."

This shakes my mother to the core and she barely hears the rest of the tour of what I will learn to do on my own. In the elevator returning to the ICU floor, my parents turn to each other in disbe-lief. "This is not for our daughter," they decide. "Surely there must be another place," as though moving me to another rehab center will change my physical state.

My father had been on the phone earlier tracking down various rehab facilities. My parents focus on Craig Hospital in Colorado, where they are told other young people, closer to my age, are abun-dant. A young man, who played high school football with Stephen, was injured in an accident and left a quadriplegic. He had been treat-ed at this Colorado facility and his father, a doctor, recommended it for me.

By the time my parents return to my room, they have decided Craig Hospital is probably my best option. My father looks shaken, which is very out of the ordinary. My mother appears very pale, very traumatized.

"We think Colorado is the best place for you," my father says. He explains his reasons.

My mother adds, "It is the best option. The facilities here…"

What are they talking about? I have everything here I need: the swimmers, my friends and everyone else at Notre Dame. I can't leave this school, these people. Medically, my parents believe it might not be the best place for me, but I know this is where I belong. This is where the story began, and this is where it has to end.

"I am not leaving South Bend," I inform them very clearly. "I am not leaving my teammates."

Their silence allows me to believe that I have won. But my parents know my spine is not stable enough for me to travel at this time. No need to fight this battle now, they think.

My mother sits down. My father heads out to make more phone calls, to get more information, and to try to make sense of it all.

The mail arrives and it is a breath of much-needed fresh air. The cards and letters are just beginning, yet each one is a welcomed and needed source of strength. My Aunt Paulette has sent a journal. On the first page it reads, "January 24, 1992. Today begins a new journey…" Over the next several months I will pour my heart out through the words I write in this journal.

Another letter comes from a rehabilitation center in Phoenix, signed by the entire staff. During my junior year at Xavier, I had a typical swimmer's injury. Ignoring the pain, I swam until I could barely lift my arm. My rehabilitation doctor thought I had ruined my shoulder. But after six months of intense physical therapy, I swam once again. This letter simply states:

"We know what you can do, Haley. Now, you show them!"

I need hope, and today, with my usual visiting hoard down to a trickle because of the funerals, hope and faith come in the mail, faith to sustain me through the pain of missing what is happening on campus and in St. Louis.

Notre Dame continues to give. Dick Rosenthal has arranged for half the swim team to fly to Colleen's funeral on several private jets. Colleen's parents did not come to South Bend. Why should they? Their daughter's body was flown home to be laid to rest.

My mother goes to Meghan's funeral and my father stays with me. I wanted to go, begged to go, but everyone denied me. Rightfully so; I am in no condition to sit up, let alone leave the hospital. But I am still disappointed and desperately want to be included.

When my mother comes back she looks beautiful, though I can see in her eyes the myriad of emotions that the funeral brought together for her: pain, sorrow, pride.

"The service was wonderful," Mom says.

She also experienced what I have tried to explain, about how South Bend, and Notre Dame, is where I belong.

"Haley, the swimmers are so amazing. Just amazing people," my mother says. "They took me right in, as if I were a part of the team. It was a huge comfort to me."

As the Mass ended and they went to bury Meghan, my mother was again reminded that we have to consider ourselves fortunate.

"I could not stop looking at Mrs. Beeler," my mother says. "I could not stop thinking; 'There but for the grace of God go I.' I wish I could somehow bring her comfort. Let her know Meghan is here with you."

The hearse carrying Meghan headed from the Basilica to the grave site, in the cemetery right by the main entrance to Notre Dame. The swim team members, wearing their swim team parkas, paraded with honor behind the hearse. My mom walked behind them with hundreds of others.

"I am so proud to have you be a part of this team," my mother says with tears in her eyes. "After the service at the grave, Coach Welsh kept the team, and everyone else left. I started to walk away, but one of the swimmers took my hand and said, 'Stand with us.' So I stood with the swim team and said a good-bye to Meghan, for you.

"I remember coming here in the fall when you started school," my mother says. "All of us were in the Joyce Center, with the new freshmen on the floor, and the parents in the stands. They talked about, 'Your children are our children now; you are a part of our family." I am sure that is a traditional thing for colleges to say. But Notre Dame doesn't just talk it; they live it and practice it."

My mother is fully grasping what I mean about the Notre Dame family.

I tell anyone who comes to visit: I will walk and swim again for Meghan and Colleen, and that I am lucky to be alive. Walking and swimming will happen here, in South Bend. This community, and particularly my school, has given me so much care, so much love, and so much of themselves. I have to give something back, and the best gift I have for them is to heal. It is all about healing now. I just have to figure out how to get those red toes to move.

Monday night is not pleasant. After everyone leaves around 10 p.m., my brother again plays *Lone Ranger* and will stay through the night with me.

Stephen and I are talking, and I feel this ache in my legs. I keep feeling this tingling sensation in my legs and feet, and it is very uncomfortable. If I could move them, I would shake it off; move them around to relieve the discomfort. But I cannot, and my legs remain stationary and achy. My brother answers the call once again, and he rubs my feet and legs. Not even a half an hour later the tingling returns and he rubs again. Whatever he is doing: the rubbing, the positive emotion he is sending me, or just the fact that he is touching me; it makes my legs feel better. I cannot feel his hands on my calves; I just feel relief.

Still, it happens again and again; sometimes once every hour, sometimes several times every half an hour. The ache is dull, but constant, and I release the painkiller to help me doze off, while my brother goes back to work rubbing. I am exhausted, but do not sleep well. Frustrated, I spend most of the night sobbing. What I do not know is that Stephen is sobbing too, but for a different reason. He is glad to stay up the entire night on call to rub my legs. By the time sunlight comes he is still standing on guard when the tingling returns, so he rubs some more.

8

When my parents arrive this morning, my brother is exhausted. He has been awake for almost 24 hours. My mother insists he go to the hotel to get some sleep.

I am about ready for a good day; any time now would be welcomed.

Last Friday began, literally 17 minutes into it, with the accident. Saturday, I learned that two of my friends died. Sunday, I was told my paralysis is permanent, and that I have to "look forward" to life in a wheelchair. Monday, yesterday, Colleen and Meghan were buried, and my parents told me they do not think South Bend is the best place for me. Monday night just ended for my brother and me, and aside from the night of the accident, it has been the worst night with the constant leg pain.

My father is leaving today. He is going home to see my sister and to settle what was unsettled when they left in the middle of the night. Mostly, of course, Mary Frances needs a parent, deserves a parent. Though I will miss my father, he will return soon and bring my sister with him. I certainly understand why he needs to go.

He is not one to cry, but I can see the emotion on his face. He does his best to stay strong for me, because he thinks that is what I need. Maybe he is right. But I would give anything to ease his pain, to lift this burden off this loving man, so I force my best smile.

"I'm going to be back very soon," he says. "And I will call every day, several times." Of course he will.

My father is standing to my right, and my mother is in her usual place on my left. She has a phone call, but asks to take it in my room, and that request is granted.

"I just don't want to leave Haley alone," she tells my father, and he nods.

The phone rings and on the line is Dick Rosenthal, Notre Dame's athletic director, who is in Kansas City on business. He was here with us the night of the accident and has given all his support and care to my parents and me, and to all the other girls on the team and their families. As conversations unfold, we will learn that Dick played professional basketball with my Uncle Ernie Vandeweghe; and that he was roommates with my Aunt Colleen's brother when their team—then the Fort Wayne Pistons—traveled. It is a small world, and one in which we continue to find goodness and friendship.

My mother turns away, perhaps to tell Dick that we have been told the paralysis is permanent, and not wanting me to hear what she is saying. She turns back toward me.

"So, yes, Dick, everything is pretty much status quo," she says.

Although my dad is beside me, I am concentrating on my feet. I am here, but not here. Dr. Klauer's words echo through my mind.

"The spine is the trunk of the tree," I hear his voice say, "and the nerves are branches, and the branches are healing, and the nerves are growing. Keep sending signals to the branches."

This is all I have done for four days, watching my feet, painstakingly telling my body to heal and sending signals. Maybe today the message will get through. The trunk is sending signals. The "branches" ached last night, and something…is happening.

Again, I look down at my feet, and my toes are propped up by a pillow. My red toes. It is time.

I see the large toe on my right foot wiggle. Slightly. I am not sure I believe what I see, so I do it again. Certain that it is moving and not taking my eyes off that toe, I squeeze my dad's hand and calmly say, "Daddy, look."

He does, and I wiggle my toe again, and again, and again for good measure.

"Charlotte!" my dad screams. He points toward my feet. "Look!"

My mother screams and jumps up, dropping the phone on the floor. She hugs me. My father holds up his hands and pumps his fists. No longer holding back tears, he hugs me too. And I move my toe again.

A small voice is yelling in the distance. It is the phone, on the floor. My mother picks it up.

"Did Haley fall out of bed?" Dick Rosenthal asks.

"No!" my mother yells, her voice full of the explosive emotion she's wanted to release since she got that phone call in the middle of the night. "It's Haley! She is moving her toe! I am looking at a miracle!"

Nurses come in and a doctor follows. There is so much noise and chaos in the room that my mother tells Dick Rosenthal she will call him back, and he insists that she does so when she has time.

"Right now," she says and he understands, "I am going to watch this miracle."

The rest of the toes on my right foot soon follow, and then my left toes. The right ankle comes to life after that.

More doctors are coming in.

"Move your foot," one says.

I do.

"Move your left big toe," another orders.

The left foot is back. Everyone is beaming, myself included.

I am going to be all right.

My mother does all she can to hold in her emotions as the nurse who told me the paralysis was permanent looks at her. She is right, and the nurse is wrong. But both are drenched in relief, and bathed in happiness.

Good news travels fast, and this news spreads like wildfire. Dr. Halperin, the attending physician from the emergency room, is suddenly here. Next comes in Nurse Shawn from Recovery. It is as loud in the hallway as it is in my room.

My father, never one to be late for a plane flight, looks at his watch.

"Haley, I have to go," he says, but he is still smiling. "This is the best present I could take with me. I love you."

"I love you too, Daddy," I say.

My mother walks him out into the hall and they are holding onto each other, savoring this moment, this corner turned and this new lease on my life. A life I am lucky to have.

Another nurse comes in with the sensation kit and the needles I never felt, not even once, even though I wanted to believe I could feel them. She starts on one foot and continues up one leg and down the other. While I still cannot feel the pin pricks on most parts of my legs, the pricks I can feel on my abdomen hurt. But it is a good pain; a pain that brings smiles to everyone. There is more hugging, more embracing of reality, which hasn't deserved much of a hug until now.

My brother comes back that afternoon. He has slept since he got to the hotel, and just woke up, ate and hurried back to the hospital. When he walks in my room he is shocked at what he sees: smiles and excitement. I tell him I moved my toes and I show him my latest trick: a slow wiggle of the toes.

"No way! I knew it! I just knew it last night when I was rubbing your legs," he says, his smile breaking out. "And then once I'm gone, you decide you need to move your toes. I see how it is!"

We laugh and he hugs me. I then realize what Stephen hoped to be true: that the aching last night was my body starting to come out of the paralysis, the effect of life rushing back into my legs.

Once the shock is gone, my brother gets upset with my mom, in an affectionate way.

"What? I stay up with her all night and no one bothers to call me to tell me the good news? Thanks a lot!" he says with a huge grin. No one can stay upset for too long right now. The mood is pure joy.

As my brother leaves to call Marcia, he reaches down and tickles my toes. I do not move.

"Did you feel that?" he asks. The panic on his face is priceless.

I smile. I am just messing with him.

"Of course," I say, as I wiggle the toes he just tickled.

"You," he says smiling, "are something else."

The doctors and nurses allow us to enjoy this time. There is no discussion of what is next. There is no talk of moving me from South Bend. On campus, as word spreads of my toes moving, swimmers and friends, and countless others, make their way back to the hospital. This time not out of respect, but to see what most of them have spent the last five days praying for.

By the end of the day, I am exhausted and my toes are barely able to move. For the first time since the meet against Northwestern, my fatigue is from hard work. It feels good. I fall asleep with a smile.

Thank you, Meghan. Thank you, Colleen.

Three more days in Intensive Care. Wednesday, Thursday and Friday all run together with more of the same: more toe wiggling, more visitors, more flowers and cards. But thankfully no more talk of leaving South Bend. I am here to stay, and hopefully not for long.

"She will be in the hospital, in rehab, for at least a year," my parents are told by Dr. Michael Long, Dr. Klauer's colleague and the physician who will oversee my rehabilitative care. One year. One year to relearn any and all function I can. Or so he says.

I am fitted for a back brace, but it is not a good fit. The brace is standard issue, but my back is oddly curved. I have a large knot the size of a fist in my upper back, which I suppose is a result of the fractures and breaks. I look like a one-humped camel. A nurse returns the brace to have a hole cut in the back in order to take the pressure off my broken spine. Sitting up will have to wait one more day. Until then, I continue to wiggle my toes, rotate my ankles and do the "rock-n-roll,' as we call shaking my legs. I quickly graduate to small leg lifts, though nothing like the ones from the Jane Fonda videos I did in high school.

Every time I do a "set" of a certain number of repetitions, I do two extra: one for Meghan and one for Colleen. My mother calls out their names to inspire me, and I have more conviction and drive for the last two repetitions. These are for my teammates who are very much still with me.

Three big Notre Dame duffel bags arrive. They have been sent by the athletic department, many of whom, like everyone else in the Notre Dame family, have checked on me several times already.

Missy Conboy, an assistant athletic director, explains the contents to me: sweats, t-shirts, shorts, socks, everything with a Notre Dame insignia. As long as I am in rehab, I am to wear Notre Dame clothing.

"You are still part of our team," she says. "You will be a Notre Dame athlete through every phase of this comeback."

This cheers me up immensely. I love wearing things with Notre Dame on them. I am part of the team, and I am very proud of that. I find a Notre Dame bumper sticker in one of the bags and ask my mom to put it on the front of my brace when it returns.

What more can they do? Not enough if you are Notre Dame. The student body president and vice-president come to visit with a get-well card, comprised of over 30 pieces of large poster board. Every dorm and building on campus has contributed a poster board to the card. In less than one week from the accident, 10,000 signatures and notes of encouragement fill this get well card. My friend Nancy has signed it several times, each time she saw it in any given building. She calls me "Ferris Bueller" because "everyone knows who you are." How could I not get better at a place like this?

Stephen is in rare form.

"You know, they are going to make a movie about this someday," he says.

I smile. Stephen being Stephen.

"Who do you think should play you?" he asks.

I think about Julia Roberts, but since we watched her in *Dying Young* the night of the accident, I think that would be too weird. I would love it if people thought I looked like her. Our hair is the same length. Maybe I will dye mine red.

So, I don't know.

"I know who is going to play me," Stephen says.

I look at him; he has obviously given this some thought.

"Me!" he says smiling.

That is probably fitting. There is only one Stephen Scott, even though there are two of them in our family alone.

9

It is Friday, exactly one week since the accident. What a week it has been.

Best-case scenario. It is a term I have heard all week and it is never a good term to hear. There is nothing "best" or even "better" about a best-case scenario. This is a term used to say, "Yes things are terrible, but maybe not so terrible." It is just not as optimistic as it sounds.

So I brew my own hope. I put in a lot of my mother, a lot of Notre Dame, and the faith of my family and friends and the community of South Bend.

And look what hope and faith have brought thus far: No longer is the best-case scenario learning how to function in a wheelchair. The thought of learning to cook or make my bed from a wheelchair did not exactly cheer me up and it sounded really hard. Now, I am heading to the rehab floor to learn how to walk again. That is better than the best-case scenario. But in my mind, it is the only acceptable one.

I am supposed to move upstairs to the rehabilitation floor this morning. However, "this morning," much like "best-case scenario," is a bit misleading. We wait for over four hours.

Mom and I pass the time by doing our "Parade of Flowers." There are too many floral arrangements to fit in my Intensive Care room, so my flowers line the counter of the nurses' station. The only time I get to enjoy them is when Mom parades them through my room, where we critique them and how they are presented. This is silly and to an outsider it might seem odd, but we have fun doing it.

My mother then learns from a nurse that I will be moved to a "double," a shared room for rehabilitation.

"That is not possible," my mother corrects the nurse.

"It is not possible for Haley to have a single room," the nurse states.

"It is not possible to have visitors in the ICU at all times of the day and night," my mother continues. She starts pulling out numbers, like my father, but human numbers, which is my mother's very own touch.

"She had 83 visitors in the ICU one day and 94 the next day. That is not possible, is it? I am here right now and it is not visiting hours," Mom says, gathering momentum. "My daughter was poked with a pin until she looked like a cactus, told she was paralyzed and then, what do you know, she is moving her toes, then her feet and legs. Not possible? Anything is possible."

A very kind older gentleman in a single room on the rehabilitation floor finds out "Haley Scott" is looking for a single room. He volunteers to pack up and head to a double. Again the impossible becomes possible.

I am moved to my single room, which is filled with flowers, cards, signs and balloons before I even get here. I am thankful not to be alone, even in a single. Angels swirl around our family day and night: The woman who comforted my mom as the sun rose in St. Louis, my teammates, my friends, the doctors and nurses, the Notre Dame family. I am surrounded by good people. And in a bad situation, the one thing you can hope for is good people.

More good people arrive when my high school swim coaches fly in that afternoon from Phoenix. A father-and-son duo, Jeff and Gerry Seaquist have coached several Arizona state-championship teams and their presence cheers me up immensely. They have brought a video camera to document their visit. I am thrilled, even excited, to record my latest feats to send back to Xavier to show my friends, my former teammates and the administration. Sister Joan Fitzgerald, Xavier's principal, has generously sent my former coaches to South Bend for a brief visit. They boost my spirits upon their arrival, and their return home with video of my progress, boosts the spirit of the Xavier community.

Another unexpected visitor arrives. Notre Dame's football coach has come to pay his respects, to brighten my day. And he does. Coach Lou Holtz is charismatic and personable, and his words of admiration and support put me at ease in his presence. Stephen's girlfriend Marcia had sent a pennant from last month's Sugar Bowl signed by Florida's football coach, Steve Spurrier. I ask Coach Holtz to sign it too. His visit and the pennant are treasured.

The next morning, my "new-and-improved" hole-in-the-back brace arrives. My nurse and a technician put the brace on me for the first time. Once tightened, they work to sit me up. It is not an easy task, as my entire body must be moved and shifted in a straight position. I do not have the ability to help at all, yet I try to, which makes it a more difficult task. Sitting, the pain is so intense I begin to feel faint, then cold, then sweaty and then…I pass out.

This brace still does not allow for the odd hump on my back. I will need a custom molded brace to accommodate my newly shaped body. Unfortunately, this will delay physical therapy for a few more days. I am disappointed because I am anxious to begin. However, I am also relieved to be able to lie down and rest for two more days. My first experience sitting up was unexpectedly exhausting and painful, especially for something that used to require such little effort.

I am tired today for obvious reasons, but also because I talked to my teammate Cara Garvey late last night on the phone. I realize after talking to Cara that she is struggling, as are a lot of girls, with the accident and how to deal with all of her emotions. Because I only see my teammates when they come to visit, wearing their best happy face to keep up my spirits, I am unable to understand how this experience is taking a toll on them, their friendships and their relationships. Survivor's guilt, making sense of the nonsensical, mourning Meghan and Colleen, and worrying about me; they have it all. And I have very few of those feelings yet. Right now I can only focus on my physical healing. The rest will come. But I am glad Cara and I had a chance to talk because it keeps me in touch with the team.

Finally, I am fitted with a brace that is tailor-made for my broken, humped back. When I put it on and sit up, I am amazed at how comfortable I am. But again, after 15 minutes, I pass out. Nevertheless, I am excited to start physical therapy.

Reality is harsh. I have no strength, even though I can see the toned muscles in my legs. I can move them, pushing with my legs and rocking from my hips, but there is no functionality to them. Parts of my legs are still numb, as is most of my back. The sensations do not return right away, and very well may never.

To begin physical therapy downstairs in the rehab room, I must first learn to get there. Transferring from the bed to my wheelchair is a process, yet one that gets easier and quicker each day. I am told I will need to learn this on my own.

"Really?" I ask. "Why?"

"Because someday you will live on your own and need to do this by yourself," a nurse answers.

No really, why? I am not going to be in a wheelchair for the rest of my life. Why does no one else know that? Learning a wheelchair transfer seems like a waste of time, especially when I can be using that time to learn how to walk. At least that is my opinion. But I am not in charge of my physical therapy regimen. First things first. Patience. If I did not have it before, which I did not, I am learning it now. This is one tool God forgot to give me beforehand. I am learning patience as I go. Or as I wait.

While transferring from a bed to a wheelchair is not as complicated as one might think, physically it is actually quite difficult. I have to use my arms to sit up and to roll my legs off the side of the bed, all while trying to keep my body in a straight-aligned position. A sliding board, which is really just a piece of wood, acts as a bridge to allow me to scoot myself across from the bed to the wheelchair. I try to understand that this is a necessary task for me to learn, or so they say, but it is pretty frustrating for me. I want to learn how to walk—not how to sit in my wheelchair. In this regard, I am not a very good patient. Fortunately, my mother is with me and seems to know my exact thoughts. She either helps me with the task when no one else is around, or reminds me that this is a temporary situation that I just need to get through.

With only an elevator ride to catch my breath before having to transfer out of my wheelchair, I am exhausted and need to rest. Then I begin what I call the real work: learning to walk.

But learning to walk is not what I thought it would be. I am devastated to learn that I cannot just stand up and walk again. What is wrong? I can see the muscles in my legs, so I know they are strong enough to carry my body. And I can move my limbs again, so I know the messages are being sent down my spinal cord. What is the problem? Why can I not just stand up and walk? It has been less than two weeks. Can a body forget how to walk in less than two weeks? Yes, it can. And mine has.

"You must retrain your body. You must learn to walk again, as you did when you were a baby," Carla Wenger, my physical therapist, tells me. Carla has visited me a few times upstairs in my hospital room. But it is here, in the rehabilitation room, where she and I will share our most intimate moments. Carla is young and small; I have no idea how she is able to pick me up or move me. But she is exactly who I need, someone who understands the skills I need to learn and who has the temperament and personality to embrace the challenge of an 18-year-old patient.

She guides me with my wheelchair transfer and demonstrates how she would like me to roll back and forth on the mat. Carla helps me do this the first few times, and it is more difficult than I think it will be. For some reason, my arms get in the way and I have trouble rolling over them. I spend the next 30 minutes struggling to do a log roll back and forth, each time pushing with my foot and flopping over with little grace. But I can do it.

With physical therapy in the mornings, lunch is a time to rest. I watch *The Young and the Restless* and usually eat a sandwich that my mom has picked up for me on her morning walk. I still do not find hospital food appealing. After lunch, the mail arrives. This is one of my favorite times of day. I have always loved getting mail and had always tried to maintain pen pals when I was younger. Each day I receive a stack of mail, sometimes 20 or 30 cards and letters. I hear from friends, family members and even complete strangers. I enjoy mail from all three. Two particular friends, Marilyn Koch and Maren Krupa, send a card each day. And on Mondays, two cards arrive from each of them. For six months, they never miss a day. Maybe because I am tired from morning therapy, or perhaps because of the kindness poured out in the heartfelt cards, each day mail time brings tears. I am overwhelmed by the love and encouragement that arrives in written form. As tired as I might be, these letters propel me through afternoon therapy.

My father returns that weekend for the first time since my toes wiggled and he has brought my sister, Mary Frances. As she enters my room I smile at this 14-year-old girl who is overwhelmed by my environment. I am glad to see her, but there is a distance. As a child on the brink of her teenage years, she is just beginning to explore her own identity; and now she is faced with the reality that everything she once knew has been changed by the fact that I am lying flat on my back unable to move. Her sister cannot walk, her mother is gone, and even when her father is with her, he is emotionally elsewhere.

Mary Frances sits next to me and I can tell she is uncomfortable, maybe nervous. I try to think of what to say or how to help her, but I struggle. It is as though the bus accident has wiped clean all prior relationships, friendships and family ties. Everything from "before the accident," a phrase we use often, has to be rebuilt, and with my sister I do not know where to begin. She has stepped into my new life two weeks too late.

My mother tries to help us make sense of each other.

"Haley, show Mary Frances what you can do," she suggests.

I wiggle my toes, rotate my ankles and rock my legs back and forth from the hip. Then my latest feat: bending my knee and sliding my heel up the bed. My right leg responds, while my left leg just flops over. My mother's face lights up with pride.

Mary Frances just stares.

"That's it?" she asks, now even more confused.

My mother is stunned and for once does not know how to respond. She wants to yell at my sister for being insensitive. But instead Mary Frances and I burst out laughing: she because she is 14 years old, and I because I understand her point of view. To her, my legs resemble nothing more than a fish out of water flapping around on the ground. As we laugh, my mother's anger relaxes and then turns to sadness. My sister is able to make me laugh; something my mother is not always able to do. Although she is so much more to me than a mother should be to her 18-year-old daughter, she feels it is never enough. My mother aches to give more.

My father has brought something else with him besides my sister: a video camera. For some reason this annoys me, although it did not when my swim coaches arrived with their video camera. With

Dad there is a fuzzy distinction between my dad the father and my dad the lawyer. I have always understood this, but in my vain and egocentric world, I am annoyed. Why would he want to record me at my worst? I look horrible. The steroids make my face break out and the "rinse-less soap" I am given to wash my face and hair cannot possibly be working. Doesn't he realize that? Why would I want video of a time in my life that I already wish to forget? He has his reasons. And as I will learn later on, I do forget most from this time and I will be very glad to have this visual reminder.

More visitors. I love this. This time it is a group of guys from the swim team. They come in, cool, cocky and cute, and they take over my room. They laugh and joke with me as if I am not in a hospital bed with a broken back. I need this. It is a bit of normalcy.

One guy puts his foot up on my hospital bed, while another leans on the rails. They tease me, make me smile, fill me in on gossip and talk about practice. One guy takes the last available chair and puts his foot up over the rail on the right side of my bed. He accidentally bumps into a plastic bag, which unknown to him, is filled with urine. The bag opens and spills out onto the floor. Slowly, one by one, each guy moves to the other side of my bed until they are all on the left side of me. Typical college guys, no one wants to address this or embarrass me—or themselves—so they continue their conversation as though nothing is running on the floor. Then, they quickly retreat with hugs, high fives and an occasional kiss on the head.

My mother, who tries to stay out of the way when I have visitors, comes in from the hallway and panics when she realizes what has happened. I am still smiling from my recent visitors, not knowing that my urine continues to seep across the floor. Mom hesitates to tell me what has happened, but she is always honest with me. I strain to look as she begins to clean it up, but then lay my head back down on the pillow, close my eyes and think, "Well, what can I do?" I try not to be embarrassed, and surprisingly, I am not. The guys will return the next day, and the next week, and each time they all stand only on the left side of my bed.

My bladder continues to be an issue. Because I am not mobile—but mainly because controlled voiding has not returned—I am still catheterized. My night nurse, Debbie, says there are thousands of people who remain catheterized their entire lives. What? No way! It is uncomfortable, and she is crazy if she thinks I will ever be able to catheterize myself. But that is where I am heading, if function does not return soon. I begin "Klauer Power," or my return to Yoda, to work on making this happen.

That night I think about how perfect my parents are for my situation. My mother is perfect for a child learning to walk again and to retrain her body, because she spends her days with preschool children who are learning to walk and train their bodies for the first time. She knows the process and understands the emotional and physical frustrations. My frustrations are similar, though perhaps more complex, than those of a 2-year-old's.

My father, on the other hand, does not have the skills to be as hands-on. His expertise lies in taking care of the behind-the-scenes logistics that allow my mom and me to operate and function as we do. He tracks down and seeks different medical opinions, handles the insurance and medical bills, and will eventually work on settling a monetary claim with the bus company to avoid a lawsuit.

For three weeks my days are filled with rehab and more rehab: physical therapy in the morning, occupational therapy after lunch and, if I am not too tired and my back is not too sore, physical therapy again in the afternoon. It is at times frustrating, and it is always repetitive and hard. But I push forward with Colleen's and Meghan's help, and with my goal in focus: to get up and walk.

Once I master logrolling in both directions on the mat, I learn to rock back and forth on my hands and knees like a toddler. And I do look exactly like a toddler; unsure if my body is ready for this, even though my mind is already racing across the room, across the campus, and toward swim practice. After a few days of practicing rocking back and forth, I start to crawl. Slowly and carefully, I move my hands and knees, lose balance, then fall. My balance is poor and I have lost all sense of proprioception: the ability to know where my body is, or where my legs and feet are, without looking at them. This deficiency will need to be overcome, especially as I prepare to stand up.

Valentine's Day slides into "today" on the calendar and I feel a bit more blue than usual. I am a college girl and I want to be someone's Valentine, which I know will not be the case this year. But the swim team and some other classmates know better. They throw me a surprise Valentine's party in one of the hospital's meeting rooms. The University's Glee Club sends out 12 singers who serenade me with songs. I know everybody has plans for later tonight, yet they still make time to spend the early evening with me. How can I feel sorry for myself when people care so much about me?

As the days go on, the visitors do not stop. Professors and administrators stop by on their lunch hours. Friends continue to come after class and swimmers arrive after practice. There is always laughter and lots of food in the room—homemade cookies, snacks—anything a visitor or hospital-bound college student would like. It is a daily afternoon open house, and I take it upon myself to help each visitor feel better when they come in. They nervously ask, "Are you feeling better?" or "Does it hurt?" I see their relief when I answer that I feel well, that I am not in too much pain and that I have improved from the day before. This uplifts everyone's spirits, and I feel as good as they do when they leave.

The few friends who see my back, the ones whom I allow a brief and gruesome glimpse of the "other side of Haley," both literally and figuratively, tend to worry more. The incisions, stitches and the nasty bump that defines my torso are a very real indication of the severity of my injury. I can hide from it at times, because I cannot see it. But for those who do, there is no denying that I have a lot of healing to do.

I am able to sit up on my own, with my brace on of course, and it feels like such an accomplishment. But I am a sprinter and a competitor and, in my mind, I am moving at a snail's pace. But I am moving, I tell myself, and that is better than lying still.

The first time I stand, I am reminded again of my injury. One would think it would be hard to forget, but I am still trying to make sense of my deficiencies. As I sit on the table mat, with my legs dangling over the side and a walker within reach, Carla asks me to put my arms around her neck. I do, and she pulls me up.

"Can you feel the pressure on your legs?" Carla asks.

I look at her, shocked. I cannot. I know I am standing because my viewpoint is higher, but I cannot feel my legs standing, nor can I stand on my own. If I closed my eyes, I would not know whether I was sitting down or standing up. It is exciting and depressing at the same time.

When I return to my room after therapy, I ask my mom to call Tim, who I know is in the middle of coaching practice.

"Tell him to ask the swimmers not to come visit this afternoon," I tell my mom. "I want to be alone."

I am too sad to entertain visitors. It is too depressing to face reality. Yet I know I need to be thankful. I do my best to honor Meghan and Colleen by keeping a good attitude. But I still have a long way to go.

In an effort to become self-sufficient, one of the first "life skills" my occupational therapist (OT) wants me to learn is to dress myself. Sue, my OT, is an intern. She is still in training, yet she is perfect for me. Her greenness is reflected only in her enthusiasm and her patience with this most-impatient patient. Getting dressed by myself is not easy. I put on my sweatpants one leg at a time and use a "grabber" to pull them up—while rocking back and forth—an inch at a time. It takes about 20 minutes for me to put on my pants. Occasionally, I practice dressing myself, though when no one is around, my mom gives in and quickly helps me dress. She knows how annoying and frustrating it is for me.

This part of therapy is not fun, and I cannot go at the pace I want. My body cannot match the speed of my mind. Not to mention the fact that I know I will never have to put on sweat pants while lying down. I know, someday, I will be standing, walking, and moving around. So why do I need to learn the logistics of this? It is frustrating. I try not to take it out on Sue, so I end up taking it out on my mom.

One of my nurses, Debbie, knows how hard this is for me, and sees how hard it is for my mother, who remains dedicated and supportive. When Debbie senses tension in my room, she often steps in, knowing I need my space and that my mom does too. I will not tell my mom to leave, and my mother would never leave me. So Debbie subtly takes over.

"Charlotte, how about I take you on a tour of the new rehab wing?" Debbie offers as more of a command than a statement. My mother is close to several of my nurses, but particularly to this night nurse.

Memorial Hospital of South Bend is building a new rehabilitation wing. I will most likely not be here when it opens, and I am sure my mom has little interest in going, but she sees it as a quick break—and I tell her to go.

She returns with few words and a renewed energy.

"Haley, I want to show you what I just saw."

It is about the last thing I want to do, but she insists. What could I possibly need to see on a rehab floor that is not even finished?

Mom wheels me to the elevator and we exit into a dimly lit hall. She moves slowly to maneuver my wheelchair through equipment and the mess of a typical construction site, yet she is moving me with purpose. I sense she knows exactly where she is taking me.

We turn a corner and she wheels me down a hallway with one hospital window at the end. She pushes me right up to the window. I look but see nothing other than the tops of a few buildings and a Pizza Hut. My mom helps me undo my wheelchair straps and I brace myself to stand and get a better view.

There, lit up in its entire splendor, I see the Golden Dome on Notre Dame's campus. The Dome, shining above the dark of the surrounding campus and neighborhood. The Dome, the first site we would see when we returned from swim meets and I would think, "We're home." And we were. The Dome, Notre Dame, home. It is so close, yet I am so far from returning.

I cannot speak. I just stand, leaning on the window sill, looking at the Dome. It watches over me. Notre Dame watches over me, a tangible reminder that God watches over me too.

Tears stream down my cheeks. I cannot hold them back, as I often do. Not tears of pain, frustration, or fear, but emotional tears. My mother sees my face and embraces me gently.

"I know this is where you belong, Haley," she says softly.

"I have to go back to my life there, Mom," I say.

"I know, Sweetie," she says. "I know."

As part of my rehab, I am required to go to group therapy with the other rehabbers. I am dreading this and I try to get out of it. But I am told it will encourage the other patients to have someone younger among them. Still, I am not looking forward to, what I think will be, a waste of my time.

I am wrong.

Sitting in a circle in our wheelchairs, we play kickball. My legs do not work as well as some of the elderly patients who have just had their knees or hips replaced, so despite our age differences, we are evenly matched. There are lots of smiles from the group, and I find myself smiling and laughing too. It is great therapy for me, even if it does little physically to help me walk again.

Another aspect of my therapy—a part I am looking forward to—takes place in a pool. A rehab pool, but a pool nonetheless. As soon as Carla mentions this possibility, I become so excited to get back in the water. But the day I am to go, the hospital is short-staffed. There is no one to drive me in the wheelchair accessible van. What? I can't go? I am so disappointed. My mom disappears. That is good because I need to be alone. I close my eyes to hold back the tears.

Several minutes later my mom marches back into my room.

"Come on, let's go. I'll help you get in your chair. If they won't drive you, I will!"

My mom knows how important it is to me to be back in the water.

But it is nothing like I think it will be.

For a swimmer who is used to diving into the water, it is humbling to be wheeled into a pool. It is small and private, thank goodness, and there is a special wheelchair to lower me down the ramp. The water is warm and the therapist carefully helps me stand up. I am standing! How come I am not that excited? I am, I guess. But it is also much different than I thought it would be. I am used to being free in the water. It is a sensation I have loved, from the pool to the ocean, since I was a child. Perhaps I thought pool therapy would include some of this freedom as well. It doesn't and it does. Just not in the way I imagined.

I look at my mom with a panicked face. "Uh-oh, Mom! I have to go!" She knows instantly what I am talking about. My bowels release. My mother helps me out of the pool and wheels me to the locker room. I am distraught and humiliated.

"No, no Haley, this is good!" my mom says encouragingly, trying so hard to find something positive in such a mess.

"No, it's not!" I say with such anger it frightens her. I look at her with real hate; hatred of the situation, of my inability to control my body, and of the fact that my mom doesn't get it. And she doesn't. How could she? She just wants everything to be okay for her daughter. So she keeps trying.

"Sweetheart, no, your body is reacting to feeling something," she says. "This is such a positive sign, a huge step. Your body felt the water and relaxed. Your body is responding to something it is not used to—yet."

She points to the floor, "This is not a big deal." Then with her hands on my legs she rubs them. "But *this* is. It is all coming back. It might not be the way you want it to, but it is coming. And we will make it work."

From where I am sitting there is a lot of work to be done, especially with the mess that is running down onto the floor. My mother, the saint that she is, cleans me up as though I am 6-months-old, helps change me into clean clothes and wheels me out of the locker room, smelling fresh as a baby—which is exactly what I feel like.

The cold air outside helps me relax. The therapy pool was warm and the events of the small, chlorine-smelling locker room only made me more heated. The cool fresh air allows me to keep in my tears. I am so sad, so depressed. I want so badly to be okay, yet sometimes it is really hard to stay positive. It is times like now when my mother's annoyingly cheery outlook is just what I need, although I am not very good at telling her that.

"Sweetheart, just think about how great that water felt, and how your body is ready to be back in the pool again." She is right, but I ignore her and do not answer.

I love this woman. I had never hoped to be like my mom when I grew up, but I am learning, slowly and sometimes unbeknownst to me, that I do. She is everything I want and need her to be, though I am unbearably hard on her at times. She absorbs my anger like a sponge and does not deflect it back at me. Even with all her own emotions and devastation, she is consistent in her patience and her love. Of all the variables in my life right now she remains, as she has since I first saw her face that afternoon after the accident, the most constant and compassionate.

The next day, the handicap van is available and there is a driver on staff for a group therapy trip to the mall. Once again I learn a lesson in humility and humanity as I am raised on the lift into a handicapped-accessible van. My mom follows us in her car and stands there waiting while I am "unloaded."

Inside the mall, Mom and I are on our own. Sometimes she pushes me and sometimes I wheel myself. I become very aware of people staring at me. Is it because they have heard about the Notre Dame swimmer who was injured? Or is it because I am in a wheelchair? It doesn't matter. I am being stared at and I do not like it. I want to yell at them, "It's just me! I am the same person even though I can't walk! Quit staring, I am normal!"

This is a huge lesson for me and I vow I will never stare at someone in a wheelchair. I am reminded of a young boy named David. I have no idea how old he was, around 7 years old perhaps, when I met him as a volunteer at Easter Seals in high school. Nancy and I used to spend one Saturday a month with physically disabled children, "to give their parents a break," according to Beth, the lead volunteer. I never understood that, but now I do. I am sure my mom could certainly use a break. David was confined to a wheelchair, and he was one of the funniest, happiest and friendliest children I had met. In my naïve and ignorant state, I remember thinking, "Wow, that is so great he can be happy in a wheelchair." Did I not learn back then that he was completely normal, he just couldn't walk? Now I get it. *I* am normal. I just cannot walk. I keep waiting for my life to return to normal. But normal or not, this is my life and it is still just me.

With all these thoughts rushing through my head the mall does not have the effect it should have on an 18-year-old college student. I should be looking at earrings, finding clearance deals and trying on shoes. As usual, one thought overrides all others: I have to go to the bathroom.

The mall has a handicapped-accessible bathroom in the

women's section of a department store. But the bathroom is hardly wheelchair friendly; the walls are narrow and I have to maneuver down to the centimeter to even get into the stall. And I have a very small wheelchair. Even the stall's handrails are not in the right place.

It is a struggle.

Why have these stalls if wheelchairs do not fit in them? It is eye-opening, frustrating and disappointing, but at least I make it in time.

Phew! I have had it with the mall and I am ready to return to the familiarity and security of the hotel. I mean the hospital. To this day, I have a funny knack of calling the hospital a "hotel."

My dad arrives the next day for his weekly weekend visit, and I am proud and excited to show him my first few steps. Leaning heavily on the walker, I am shaky at first and cannot go far. My feet barely leave the ground and my steps are small. Carla follows closely behind with my wheelchair for when I need to rest. One step, four steps, they are slow and carefully calculated.

But I am walking. It has been a process and I am so focused on where my feet are that I do not even recognize that a miracle is taking place. My first steps. My mom has the video camera. I am taller than the camera's viewfinder, so she rotates the camera to one side as though she is taking a vertical picture and needs the height. We will laugh later as we watch me walk on my side.

10

One month. It is my brother's birthday, but there is more to celebrate. I say goodbye to the wheelchair. I have two days to steady myself before returning to campus for Ash Wednesday Mass. The swim team is getting ready for the end-of-season MCC (Midwestern Collegiate Conference) Championship meet. It is a team tradition to attend Mass before each meet. It just happens to be Ash Wednesday.

On leave from the hospital for the afternoon, I attend Mass in Dillon Hall, a dorm on campus, and sit next to Scully and Lorrei. As I walk toward the priest to receive ashes, I have to focus on each step I take. Walking, even with a walker or cane, is not easy and each step is carefully placed. But I misread the location of my foot and trip on the rug. I grab the priest's hand and thankfully do not fall. Sometimes God is obvious in His care.

The team dinner after Mass has me feeling more optimistic. I am thrilled to once again be hanging out with my friends and to hear the latest gossip and antics taking place. Yet, I am so out of the loop that the words and stories make no sense to me. I have no context for what it is they are laughing at and talking about, so I smile to hide my confusion and sadness.

Roger, a senior swimmer, asks if he can take a picture of Lorrei and me.

We stand up for the picture and exchange a look. Lorrei and I are thinking the same thought: The last time we posed for a picture together was the *Three Amigos* photo with Meghan before Christmas break. Lorrei and I smile for Roger, but there is an eerie feeling because one of the *Amigos* is not here, and won't be in a picture with us again. The sadness hits hard and our silence speaks the words we cannot fathom expressing to anyone, even each other.

This weekend at the MCC Championship meet at Notre Dame,

I hold my first press conference with the South Bend NBC and ABC affiliates, and a reporter and photographer from the *South Bend Tribune*.

The reporters ask me about my recovery and the accident. I smile and speak with optimism because that is what everyone wants to hear, even me. But when they ask about Meghan and Colleen and the grand jury investigation into the accident, I do not know what to say. I am not prepared for the latter topic. I ignore the question about the grand jury investigation, mainly because all I know is the fact that it is taking place, and I answer the question about Meghan and Colleen.

"I think about them all the time. They are always with me," I say. "The swimmers swim for them, and I walk for them."

I feel the tears begin to come, and the reporters respectfully thank me and leave.

I am glad that is over.

To have people interested in my life is so weird for me. I am just a college freshman who wanted to walk again and who wants to swim again for Notre Dame.

Most of all, I really want to swim this weekend. I love being at the pool and seeing the team. But not competing in the meet, and not being able to share in their excitement, leaves me on the outside looking in.

February turns into March and my last week of physical therapy is very independent. I practice walking with the cane, though I hate using it and I try to get by on my own when no one is looking. From my hospital bed to the bathroom is an easy trip: I hold onto the end of the bed, take two steps to the side table, one step to the bathroom door and I am in! No cane needed. Medically I am considered "self-sufficient," which is a strange term for an 18-year-old, but one I am becoming used to in reference to me. I can dress myself (although my mom still helps me sometimes—don't tell!), I am mobile, I can perform basic life-skills and I can navigate myself around the practice kitchen located on the rehabilitation floor.

Each day is filled with one trip outside the hospital. I visit campus to meet with my professors about upcoming school work and class time missed. I attend my last session of pool therapy, which goes much better than the first; however walking back and forth, and waving my arms back and forth in the water is still not my idea of "being back in the pool." I go to the early bird special at a steak-house buffet with my friends in group therapy. No van this time; my mom is allowed to drive me. Dinner proves more challenging than I think it will be. Once again my mom and I spar. She insists on try-ing to carry my tray of food to the table, but I convince her that I am going to have to do it alone once I am back on campus. The thought of me walking unaided in the dining hall without her, sends a whole new wave of fear through her body. She is not ready to let go.

My mother is becoming an issue. She is driving me crazy, although I am probably not being fair to her. I demand that she tell me every detail she sees when she walks around campus, and each story she hears from her talks with the hospital staff. I insist on knowing word-for-word her conversations with anyone from Notre Dame, or anyone she talks to on the phone. Yet, I shut down when she asks me to share my thoughts or my conversations with friends or teammates. She tries desperately to share in my world, and I let her in when she has information for me. But just as quickly, I shut her out. My dad comes and goes, so I am able to enjoy him when he is here, but my mom never leaves and at times I want her to. On the other hand, I would be lonely—and at times helpless—without her. Who else would sit with me for hours and not say a word? Who else would drive me to pool therapy? Who else would encourage me, but also allow me to cry? She lovingly puts up with my moods, but there are times when I want her to leave, and that makes me feel guilty.

At least I am getting more and more "alone" time. Tonight, the doctors give me an overnight leave of absence from the hospital to spend the night in Lyons Hall. I am so excited! My mom drives me to campus, and on the way to my dorm we stop in the library lobby to see a memorial for Meghan and Colleen. It is moving and inspir-ing. Built like a tunnel, people have written and posted their memo-ries of my deceased teammates inside. I walk through slowly and my mom gives me some space to view it alone. I read what others have written, but I have no idea what to write myself. Finally, I retreat to the familiar and write the truth that sounds so cliché: these incredi-ble young women are still with me, they have helped me learn to walk again and they will never be forgotten. The memorial is touching and the pictures of Meghan and Colleen so accurately reflect them. I am sure if I read all the memories I would find that the tributes do too. I am glad to have seen this, yet at the same time I wish there was no need for a memorial.

In Lyons Hall, Sister Kathleen has taken great care to recreate my second-floor dorm room in what had been the first-floor study lounge. Stairs are not a daily option for me, so the study lounge will have to do. Thankfully, everything is in place when I arrive, including my roommate Alisha. It is the same, but it's not. A reflection of me: the same, but different. I am not as happy as I thought I would be to spend the night on campus. I am worried. Worried that I might get hurt, frightened to be on my own and uncertain what life will be like once I am out of the cocoon that is the hospital. I was so excited for the one-night pass from the hospital to go back to the life I had. But that life does not exist, and this reality hits me hard.

Tonight in the dorm, and again when I return to the hospital, I have difficulty sleeping. The tingling in my legs from the nerve damage is so strong and so annoying that it hurts. I can do little but cry and try to rub them. But they still ache and I am exhausted and frustrated. Dr. Klauer prescribes something, but it does not work. Despite taking four sleeping pills, I am wide awake. I want to curse at my legs, but I cannot because I am so thankful that they even work. The tingling, coupled with my lack of sleep, is beyond irritating.

11

Discharge day! I am ready to run (if I could) out of here, but hospital procedure dictates that we must first have a family conference with my doctors and physical therapist. Carla warns me to take it easy. Knowing me as well as she does, there is a mix of pride and worry on her face. I have become one of her favorite patients, and she feels protective. Over the last six weeks she has watched me push myself and I sense that she fears I will overdo it once I am beyond her watchful eye. I promise to heed her words, and as I sit across from her, I mean it.

Dr. Klauer stops in with my most recent set of X-rays. They look pretty cool. I had seen my X-rays from before surgery where my vertebrae were crushed, but this set shows my spine, cleaned up considerably, and my rods. Dr. Klauer shows me where the bone grafts are, but it is the rods that draw my attention. They are bigger than I realized. Two large, dark rods—about the width of a thick pencil—navigate about seven inches along either side of my spine.

Most noticeable to my mother, however, is the curvature of my spine. While most of us were tested for scoliosis when we were younger, and are familiar with that medical term, my curvature is called kyphosis. Scoliosis curves right and left while kyphosis curves front and back. Basically, my spine is not straight. I am still humpbacked. Because I cannot stand without my brace, I have had to rely on my mom's daily descriptions of what my back looks like. She has been delicate in her words, but the pictures do not lie. My spine is curved forward at a 23-degree angle. She fears for my quality of life with such a hunched spine and delicate spinal cord.

One last question for Dr. Klauer before he leaves. My mom asks him about a mark on my back, a small bruise about a half an inch from my incision. Dr. Klauer looks at the bruise on my back and then looks at the X-rays.

"See here?" he asks, pointing to the picture on the X-ray light, "it is just a little bone chip."

This satisfies my curiosity, but it does not alleviate my mother's concern. My desire to be "well" and "normal" is as blinding to me as the fact that I cannot see my back for what it is. My mother knows better. Call it instinct, or her overprotective tendency to worry, but the doctor's comments do not sit well with her. However, she lays it aside, not wanting to upset me on discharge day.

I check out of the hospital as though I am leaving a hotel. This is a much bigger event than I thought it would, or wanted it to be. Nurses, doctors and staff members from every "initial" in the hospital—the ER, the OR, the ICU, PT and OT—and from the shortened and nicknamed units, Recovery and Rehab, all stop by to say good-bye and wish me good luck. They are all thrilled I am doing so well, yet seem a bit sad and sorry to see me leave. So does my mom. But I am not. I cannot wait to get out.

"Leaving all these wonderful people is so hard," my mom says. They were to her what she was to me: unwavering in their care and compassion and letting her snap at them because she could not snap back at me.

Still, I look at her like she is crazy. It is not the first time I have given her this look. For me, it is not hard leaving this place. They may be wonderful people, but I am ready to leave so I can move on with my life. I sign my own discharge papers. This time my signature is legible.

As we ride down the elevator, my mom is already talking about coming back to visit the friends we have made here. Again, crazy. All I can think about is how I never want to be in a hospital again. Ed Ballotts, a photographer from the local newspaper, snaps pictures of me walking slowly out of the hospital in my bulky brace. He takes one of Dr. Klauer and me hugging that will grace the front page of tomorrow's *South Bend Tribune*. I get in the car, smile and rip off the hospital ID bracelets. Mr. Ballotts again records this on film. I cannot wait to see these pictures.

When we pull away from Memorial Hospital, the emotions I held inside and kept from almost everyone are released. The tears begin slowly, but it is not long before I am sobbing. My mom, for once, lets me be. She cannot do much else because she is driving. In the odd world of an 18-year-old girl, I am grateful my mom is here. But I need this moment to myself to cry tears of sadness, tears of relief, tears of sorrow and tears of joy. All these emotions flow in the tears running down my face.

Although we had not talked about it, my mom knows the one place I want to go before we head to the airport for our flight to Phoenix. She drives toward campus. We turn down Notre Dame Avenue and I look to see the Golden Dome in front of us. The Dome. The Dome that seemed so far from the hospital window looms right in front of me. It is inspiring and comforting. We then make a quick left turn down a narrow driveway into Cedar Grove Cemetery. I feel the heaviness of sobs in my chest and start to cry again. I shake and am nervous with anticipation. I have wanted to visit Meghan's gravesite for weeks, yet now I am scared. I do not understand death, especially the finality of it, no matter what my faith has been or is becoming. People are only supposed to die young in movies. I have so many emotions and feelings with nowhere to put them, and no guideline to deal with them.

Meghan's grave sits right next to the road. I get out of the car carefully and walk the five or six steps to her side. My mother waits respectfully in the car. I cannot grasp that her body is in the ground. It just does not make sense to me. I see her face and it is as if I can reach out and touch it. I see her long blonde hair and her smile that brought all eyes in the room toward her. I think of her personality that I envied so much. Meghan was so full of life. How can that life not exist on this earth any longer?

There is no headstone yet, just the outline of where she was buried. I wonder what Colleen's grave looks like. I try to think of what it must have been like on the day of their funerals. My mom's descriptions of Meghan's service fill my head, but it is too hard. So I think again about the friends that I knew: Meghan who danced in the showers and had such a distinctive bounce in her walk, and Colleen who was always taking pictures. But that is hard also.

"I am walking for you," I say for my benefit, because Meghan and Colleen already know. "Thank you. Thank you for helping me through this. Thank you for helping me walk again. I will never forget you." I talk slowly and mouth the words more than speak them.

Whenever I am asked about my recovery, I talk about how Meghan and Colleen are always with me. Talking about them and to them, and asking them for help, is such a positive way to keep them in my life. But now, being physically so close to where Meghan is, I miss her so much. It becomes so real. The last time I saw her, she was smiling, wearing her Walkman and singing "OPP" or Blues Traveler, talking about a boy who is probably right now in class or at practice. But she is not. She is right here. It is hard to accept and move on. I can't. Not yet.

All of us on the swim team remember them in our own way and carry them with us, and I know at times they carry us. We all have treasured memories: the *Three Amigos*, the fun at practice, the shower and locker room talk, everything. But what most of us mourn are the lost memories that were yet to come. We were just getting to know each other, to *really* know each other. And I cry for everything we will miss sharing, for the friendships which were cut short. It is not fair. For the first time I begin to feel the unfairness of the accident.

To calm myself, I say the only Catholic prayer I know by heart, "Hail Mary, Full of Grace…"

My mom watches from the car and wishes she could comfort me. Her heart aches for me, but her tears are for Mrs. Beeler and Mrs. Hipp. As difficult as my life has been over the past two months, my mom knows she can still give me a hug.

I plant some yellow spider mums tied with blue and gold ribbons, and tell Meghan I will be back soon.

I get in the car and my mother touches my shoulder gently. I wonder if I am cold to the touch. My mother would love for me to share my feelings, but I do not. I cannot, because I do not know exactly what they are, or how to verbalize them. Plus, I just do not feel like talking. My mom wants to help. She is my mom and right now my closest friend, even though perhaps she shouldn't be. But my life in general isn't as it should be. I just sat next to my teenage teammate's grave. It is just not right.

We drive out of the cemetery in silence. Sometimes there are no words to comfort.

Winning my first swim trophy at age 8, before I started swimming competitively, at Eldorado Country Club in Indian Wells, CA, while visiting my grandparents.

Learning to swim and practicing my racing start at age three.

I won my first state championship in the 50-meter freestyle in Yuma on the day of my 11th birthday.

My brother, Stephen, and I were competitive from an early age. Here we are getting ready to race in our backyard pool in Phoenix, while Mary Frances and my best friend Nancy Martin watch from the steps.

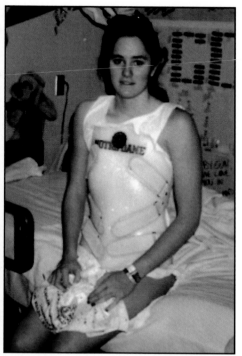

I was able to tolerate sitting up only after a hole was cut in the back of the brace to provide relief.

Doing physical therapy with Carla Wenger, I had to retrain my body to roll over, kneel and crawl, before I could learn to walk.

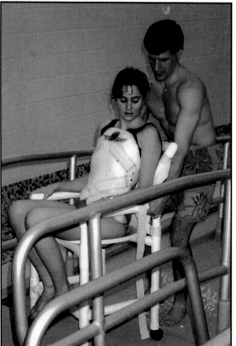

This was my first day of pool therapy in South Bend. Unable to walk, I had to be wheeled into the pool for safety.

Supporting myself standing with a walker in my decorated room on the rehabilitation floor.

Back on campus, Lorrei (left), Angie (middle) and I drove around campus but it was one more way in which my life was "not normal."

A banner made by students that hung on campus immediately following the bus accident.

A frequent bedside supporter, Susan "Scully" Bohdan visited daily in South Bend, and again visited while I recovered in California.

Mom and my brother Stephen pay me a visit. She has on her "Delicious" sweatshirt that became her nickname on the swim team.

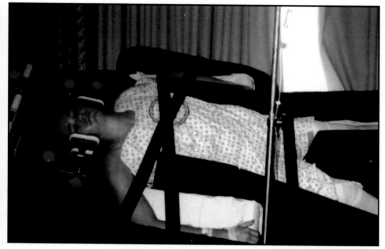

San Diego. I spent almost two weeks strapped into the RotoBed, tilting back and forth to prevent pressure sores. My legs, arms and torso were separated by panels, while my head was held stable in a halo-type apparatus.

Nancy Martin spent several weeks with me at my Uncle's condo in Del Mar, CA, while I was recovering. I was rarely allowed to leave the couch, but she kept me looking my best. That's what friends are for!

Surrounded by media in the spectator galley, Mom and Stephen watch me walk to the starting block for my first race.

Celebrating with Coach Tim Welsh after the 50-yard freestyle.

This is one of my favorite pictures. A hug from my dad after competing says it all.

Ann Hipp, Colleen's mom, cheered me on during my first race in October 1993. We shared an emotional hug after the 50-yard freestyle, and she brought along her own hand-made sign.

Running the Los Angeles Marathon in March 1997. My parents with many other family members came to watch. I finished!

I was presented the Spirit Award by Notre Dame Athletic Director Dick Rosenthal at halftime of the 1992 Michigan game.

My family cheered me on as I participated in the 1996 Olympic Torch Relay, carrying the Olympic flame in Phoenix.

Jamie DeMaria and me shortly after we got engaged in 1999. Marrying Jamie was a blessing in my life.

Dancing with Dr. Garfin, my back surgeon from the UCSD Medical Center, at my wedding in 2000.

In the South Bend Airport, wearing my Notre Dame swimming sweatshirt and walking with my cane, I am recognized and stopped by many people.

"I prayed for you." And, "I am so glad to see you walking." "What an honor to meet you!" "Can I shake your hand?" "You are a miracle."

I am always surprised and then humbled by the goodness of strangers. Their words are kind and genuine, and I know they want to hear how well I am doing and that their prayers worked. I smile and thank them and tell them that yes, in fact, their prayers did work. It is all sincere and true, but trying to smile on the outside only adds to the suffering and pain I keep inside.

I am in a fog. I need to leave for a while. The timing is perfect: Spring Break. Everyone else is gone from campus, so I will not miss out on anything while I am in Arizona. Home. I have to get home, if for nothing else, just to not always have to smile on the outside.

It is so great to be home in Arizona with Dad, Mom and Mary Frances. And while there is no doubt my life has changed here as much as it did in South Bend, being home provides a calm peace of mind.

When I am alone or in bed I talk to myself about what has happened. I do not know why I do this. I guess I just want to hear the words to figure out if they make any sense. I do not even know if I like talking about the accident. However, I must, because I talk about it all the time. Except when my mom wants to, then I don't. My poor mother, why am I so mean to her?

If other people are around, I do like talking about the accident and my surgeries because those are facts of which I can make some sense. I can talk about them objectively, clinically, and with little deep-felt emotion. The little stories and anecdotes from my time in the hospital are like pieces of a puzzle. When I listen to myself speak about them, I try to fit them together to make sense of this puzzle that is my life. But there are missing pieces, like Meghan and Colleen, and on a lesser but personal note, walking and swimming and being a normal college student. Some of these will never be found, and I need to manipulate each piece of the puzzle to find an alternative solution.

At times I find myself wondering if all this retelling is good or even healthy for me. Will I always give people the "long version" when they ask? I don't know. It is hard to tell the story in just a few minutes, but how long will everyone be willing to listen? Maybe they aren't willing now, but at least they are polite. I am sure someday this will be out of my system and I won't talk about it any longer, because I will not have anything left to say.

Heidi Fogelsong visits from Channel 3, Phoenix's ABC affiliate, to conduct an interview. She asks about the accident and my rehab, about Meghan and Colleen. She hopes to share with her audience how much I appreciate the support I received from the Arizona community, and I regurgitate the positive answers I have given before in public or aloud to myself when I am alone. She also asks me about my future plans.

"I know this will all be over when I can swim again."

This answer surprises Ms. Fogelsong and she questions it, "You are already thinking of competing again?"

I smile. "I have been thinking of competing since the day after the accident."

Heidi returns the favor and catches me off guard when she asks, "Do you still talk to your friends?"

My tone changes.

"I do," I say solemnly, "I talk to both of them."

My voice trails off and I cut my thought short because I do not want to cry. Not again. Not in front of the camera. Her question leaves me shaken. Honesty and candor knock down one of the many emotional walls I have unknowingly built. Heidi senses this and asks me to walk for the camera. I stand up with my cane and walk across our living room. I hate the cane, but I will smile and use it for now.

Heidi leaves, and while she is gracious and grateful, I have no idea if I have given her enough information for the piece she will file. I have not yet mastered the art of concise and complete thoughts, or "TV answers." But I will.

Dad and Mom spend the next two hours in the living room talking to Mary Frances, which gives me a chance to lie down. I am exhaust-ed from the interview, both physically and emotionally. My little sis-ter struggles with everyone and everything that has been heaped upon her in this whole mess. She tells them that I still get all the attention and making a mature, intuitive leap, she points out that this proves I really am my parents' favorite child.

She too is angry: angry at the situation, angry at me for being the focus of my parents' attention, and angry for taking that attention away from her. She then feels guilty about her anger. She knows this is not my fault, but she blames me anyway. While I feel badly for Mary Frances and how her life has been turned upside down, I am amazed at her strength and I envy her self-confidence.

At just 14 years old she also has been dealt this tragedy. And I, as the focal point of her concern, can offer nothing to help her or provide solace. But my parents have to try. Each of us has our unique circumstances and issues to deal with and sort through. I do not understand what Mary Frances is experiencing, just as she can-not make sense of my confusion and anger. We are all living through this nightmare together, literally now in the same house, though the distance between us at times seems like miles. Will the gaps close? Only time will tell.

I am so tired I cannot imagine getting up. Thankfully, I am able to sleep in later at home than I did in the hospital. My legs continue to ache during the night, leaving me sleepless, restless and often times angry. Today I am to visit Paradise Valley Country Club to swim with my first coach, Joe Phillips. My aunt arrived from New York City last night, so she will join us while Channel 3's television crew films me swimming in the pool.

The water feels so amazing on my body, as does the sun. Underneath my swim suit I wear my back brace. It takes a few min-utes for the water to trickle beneath my brace and it tickles as it hits my skin. What a great feeling! Still, my entire torso is encapsulated by white plastic, with only a skimpy, navy blue training suit to cover it. I look ridiculous. Although I am usually so far beyond vanity when it comes to my body, I am conscious of the brace and how I will look on camera. Still, swimming freestyle and backstroke is the best therapy for both my physical and mental state. There are very few places I relax as much as I do in the water.

Gliding so comfortably through the pool I trained in for years confirms my belief that swimming has prepared me for this challenge. Swimming is such a unique sport. You dive in the water and swim thousands of yards with your team, but each swimmer is very much alone, with only the black line along the bottom of the pool for company. Swimming requires so much internal motivation, not just for the workouts themselves, which are considerable, but to keep pushing when your body has very little left to give. Swimming is a sport of constant plateaus, valleys and the occasional peak. No athlete performs personal bests at each competition, swimmers especially. Still, you push through the plateaus, and one day, you improve and swim faster. It is such a physical and emotional challenge. Athletes work toward short-term goals every day, and those eventually add up to the long-term goal of swimming a fast time at a big meet. The swimming life was exactly the preparation I needed to deal with this challenge.

But it is more than that. It is not a coincidence that swimmers are good people and good students; the commitment and discipline that applies to our sport also applies to our lives and academic work. A swimmer takes instruction constantly and has to be willing to adapt. A good attitude is essential, especially when struggling in workout or competition. Even in an individual sport, any negativity can bring down your teammates, just as it would affect another member of group therapy or a sibling. Swimming requires you to intellectualize your goals and the steps needed to get there, just as you would in academic life. It allows you to compete not just against others, but against yourself, as you try to reach your own potential. There are some things in life, as in sport, that you cannot control. All we can do is focus on the things under our control and use them to prepare for life as it happens around us. This does not mean accept fate. It means create fate. Establish a life that prepares you for life. Surround yourself with the tools, the people and the discipline to navigate the roadblocks life puts in your way. It can happen in many ways, but for me swimming is that life.

My body is in decent shape as I move through the pool. The

strokes come easily enough, but still the brace is awkward. I cannot do flip turns as my plastic body does not bend. But at this time, just being in the water and being able to "swim" is an improvement from my time at pool therapy. I am grateful for this small, or perhaps huge, step forward. I hope it tires me out enough so that I am able to sleep well tonight.

I feel a small concentrated pressure in my back. It has been there before, and sometimes I notice it more than others. But after acknowledging it, I endure it and try to forget about it. Sort of like the cameras following me back and forth in the pool, and my mother who follows me throughout the day to make sure I am okay.

12

I am back at Notre Dame. Spending Spring Break at home was great and needed, but nothing compares to being back with my friends, especially when I am given a golf cart to drive around campus. But strangely enough, and despite knowing that this is where I belong, I felt a lot of emotions when I left Arizona. Perhaps I was sad to leave, or maybe I was scared to return. It was an odd feeling that I cannot yet decipher.

My mom traveled with me and will stay in South Bend for a week. So, while I have returned to campus and classes and to the pool, I still have not returned to an independent college life.

I continue with three classes, but only math challenges me. Fortunately my professor, Dr. Wong, is as understanding as the rest of campus. If needed, I am allowed to drop my math class, without penalty, up until the day of the final exam. I think I can manage, but this enables me to work at my own pace without additional stress.

My Freshman Seminar teacher is just as understanding and generous. I am asked to present a paper about the accident and my recovery. I spend hours working on this: making a timeline for my classmates to follow, gathering and putting together visual aids with pictures and newspaper articles, and preparing notes for my 90-minute presentation. This is the only topic on which I have the attention span to focus for more than five minutes. In a time before computers and PowerPoint, it is actually a time-laborious project.

While presenting to the 12-student seminar class, I am very mechanical in my description of the accident. Because I do not remember much beyond what I am told and because the emotions are still so raw, I talk in a very matter-of-fact voice and at an emotional distance that allows me to share my most intimate story. The students pay close attention, and many have tears in their eyes, as though I am bearing my soul. I continue to refer to it as "my accident," but I see on their faces that I am wrong. This is their accident too. It happened to their friends, their classmates, perhaps to their roommates. It affected their campus and their lives. In a community like Notre Dame, the accident was not an isolated event, affecting only those on the bus. Many students attended the Memorial Mass on January 24th, and most can tell you where they were when they first heard about the accident. They know that Notre Dame cancelled all athletic events that weekend, for the first time since President Kennedy was killed. Yet today, as my classmates listen to me describe the events of the past seven weeks, they are unaware of how deep my emotions run, of how this accident has changed me to the core. They have no idea that I keep my most personal thoughts to myself, to my journal. They hear the facts, and those are compelling enough. But I am not ready, nor able, to share the rest. In many ways I myself am unaware of the depth of my conversion.

Still, even on the surface it is strange to retrace the steps of what happened, to walk down that road again, when I still cannot walk that well myself. Did I really go through all that? At times, I find it surreal and strange to think about.

The afternoon class exhausts me and I spend the rest of the day in my dorm room, dozing in and out of sleep. I loosen the straps on my brace while I am lying down. It feels good to be free from the confines of a shell. My torso is damp from sweat, and the undershirt I wear sticks to my itchy body. I smell an odd mix of plastic and perspiration. It does not smell bad, just distinct. Sometimes the brace is so tight it is hard to breathe. If it doesn't remind me that I am not healed yet, it does remind others. I do not need to be reminded. I feel it every day, every hour, with every trip to the bathroom and every ache in my back.

It is during these times, when I am tired and drained and perhaps moving towards depression, that I retrain and refocus my thoughts to the positive. Sometimes I reread encouraging letters. Sometimes I think about how grateful I am for the efforts Notre Dame has made to ensure my comfort. As much as my first-floor dorm room represents the fact that stairs are too difficult for me, I am thankful for my new room. It is also closer to the restroom, which is becoming increasingly important. While it was a struggle to get my bladder to work in the first place, and while I am thankful that I am able to void on my own, I still have to go to the bathroom several times an hour. It is annoying, and I am familiar with the location of every bathroom in each building on campus. The golf cart helps too; we nicknamed it "Number Two" because of the large "2" on the front. Normally used for injured football players, the athletic department has issued me a golf cart to drive around campus. This is a huge hit with my friends, sometimes literally.

With only three classes, I have more free time than my classmates, teammates and friends—most of whom are all three. Some days I pick up Lorrei and Angie after class and we drive to South Dining Hall for lunch. One afternoon, they come running out of the Arts & Letters building, O'Shaughnessy (or O'Shag), and jump on the golf cart.

"Go! Go!" Lorrei yells.

Their teacher, Father Banas, just finished class by telling a story about a young woman who ran him over with a golf cart the night before. He jumped off the path into a puddle of mud, and was surprised that the young woman did not stop to see if he was okay.

I am horrified. I know exactly what happened, but I was unaware that he fell in the mud. Returning from the Freshman Year of Studies office the night before, I was driving around the Main Building, under the glow of the Golden Dome. Coming around a corner I almost ran into someone, surprising him and myself at the same time. But since I did not hit this person and because I had to go to the bathroom, I kept on driving.

"Sorry about that!" I turned my head and yelled back as I sped away, unknowingly leaving Father Banas behind in the mud.

Again, I am mortified to hear his side of the story. But seeing Lorrei's smile and hearing her and Angie laugh, I am comforted to learn that even Father Banas himself was able to laugh about it.

In the dining hall we run into Chuck Wolzack, a freshman diver on the team. I know it is him because he is the only one who approaches me from behind and "feels me up." He laughs and makes silly groaning noises as he gropes the turtle brace where my breasts should be (or are, but they are covered with a half-inch thick piece of plastic). It is funny the first couple of times, and if you have not seen him do it before, it is hilarious. With a continuous new audience, he continues to do it. That's just Chuck.

I spend a little time at the pool, and in the pool, but mostly I am too tired to swim. I have out-patient physical therapy three times a week at an off-campus rehab facility. My physical therapist is pregnant, so it's a good thing she does not have to move or lift me like Carla did. My mom drives me the first week after Spring Break. After that, I negotiate rides (although they are happy to help) from Sister Kathleen and Amy Lutz, a senior in my dorm who will attend physical therapy school in the fall. Mostly I work on balance and leg strength. It is not as hard as PT was in the hospital, at times it is boring and the results are rarely noticeable. But it is necessary for fine-tuning my body and balance, and exhausting nonetheless.

Time to visit Dr. Keucher. It has been two weeks since I was discharged from the hospital.

I undergo a series of X-rays and learn that the angle of my spine has bent forward from 23 degrees to a 30-degree angle. Although Dr. Keucher claims this is "not too significant," the reality is my back is not healing properly. I still hope my brace will come off in May, but if my back continues to collapse, Dr. Keucher states I will need an additional operation to straighten my spine. Actually, either way he recommends surgery in the future, not only to improve the structure of my back, but to improve the quality of my life.

I am surprised. I either did not expect to hear this, or maybe like everyone else, I only want to hear good news. But I look at this man, this very serious surgeon who has enjoyed my progress as his own and taken pride in my success, and I trust him. He knows my back better than anyone and if he thinks he needs to fix it, then I trust he will.

But Dr. Keucher surprises me again when he says he won't do it. He wants the best for me and there are others who are more experienced in the delicate operation I might require.

Unbeknownst to me, my mom immediately calls my dad and tells him to begin the search to find a surgeon to correct my spine.

Colleen Hipp's family travels to South Bend for the first time since her death to celebrate a Mass in her honor. My mom has stayed in South Bend to attend, and I too am looking forward to honoring my friend in this way. For some teammates it brings up feelings of anger and loss, and it reminds all of us that we need to heal as a team, as well as individually. Our sense of loss is staggering, indescribable, even intolerable. We are trying to move on. Some of us have healed, some of us have more healing to do, and some of us will never heal. What we all need to learn is that these discrepancies in healing are okay.

Gathered as a team, emotions rise and each of us look around at the collective and varied degrees of healing. No one should be blamed for their method, but we judge regardless. For some of us that too is part of the grieving process.

I meet Mr. and Mrs. Hipp tonight for the first time. I am taken by how much Colleen resembled her parents. They are so kind and so gracious, yet their red-rimmed and wet eyes display how deeply they hurt. Colleen's siblings are also here and I think of my own siblings: my brother in Atlanta who is so supportive, and my sister at home, not able to understand my life. I wish she could understand enough to be thankful that I am alive. Maybe she does. But maybe, like all of us, she does not know how to express it.

Notre Dame President Father Malloy presides over the Mass and I cannot stop crying. At church and alone at night are the two places where I find myself the most upset. Perhaps that is when I feel closest to Meghan and Colleen. Or perhaps that is when I am most able to let down my guard. I sit next to Amy Bethem and she is crying too. I am thankful. In a strange way it is easier and comforting to be around those who hurt as I do, who miss them as I do, who understand the loss. I do not have to keep my emotions in check around my teammates. There is healing in crying together.

My mom leaves the next day. For all the complaining I do about her, and to her, the idea of being apart sounds a lot better until it is time for her to leave. Then I miss her terribly. Tears well up in my eyes as she hugs me good-bye. I recognize the irony: the first time she left last August, it was I who made fun of her for crying. I try to make this easier on her, easier on us, and stay strong, but there is a void when she leaves that is filled by no one. The space I claim to need when she is here becomes a vast island of isolation. I feel very alone. I feel like no one understands what I live with. Others may understand the sadness I feel about Meghan and Colleen, but only my mother understands my moods and the complexities of my life. Yet in a way, this is my choice. I do not want to burden anyone with my pain and depression, so I hide it and it exhausts me. With my mom, there is no hiding. It is a blessing and a burden we share.

The sense of loss I feel for Meghan and Colleen has not subsided. I cannot stop thinking about them. I wonder if they are okay. I talk to them, and that helps, but will that always be enough? I have a faith strong enough to know that they are in a better place. But where does that leave us—those who are left behind? If it is such a better place, why does it hurt so badly and why do I miss them so much?

I think of my Aunt Nancy, whose faith is so strong, and who believes I am blessed to have been touched by God's love in a very real way at such a young age. I try to feel lucky to be alive and to be walking, but I often don't and I feel guilty about that. The depression hits me so hard that at times I am simply inconsolable, and to those around me, particularly my mother, I must be intolerable. How much longer will I need such a wide emotional berth to pass the days, weeks and months? Will the pain be the same next year? It is hard to imagine it will get better. Yet, as horrible as I feel asking these questions, I feel even worse when I think of the Beelers and the Hipps, because Meghan and Colleen are not here to console. I feel the most sadness for their families.

Tonight, as I do each night, I fall asleep talking to and thinking about Meghan and Colleen. I am desperate to know if they are all right.

I dream about Meghan. I am somewhere I do not recognize, but there is music playing, people dancing and it is crowded. Then I see her, across the room. She does not say anything and she does not walk towards me, but everyone else seems to fade away until I see only her face. She looks at me and smiles. There is a peace about her and I relax. It is as though she is saying, "Yes, I am all right."

I wake up, and for the first time since the bus accident, I feel at peace. She *is* okay. She is in a better place. Again in death as in life, she has inspired me, and I go about my routine today with extra effort and dignity for Meghan and Colleen.

I will never forget the look of peace on Meghan's face in my dream.

13

Two months since the accident. I walk to Rolfs Aquatic Center with Lorrei and Angie, and I swim about 500 yards in my turtle shell. It feels great to be back in the pool, back in *my* pool. The smell of chlorine and the exhilaration of the cold water are topped only by the camaraderie and warm water I enjoy in the showers afterwards, again in my brace. Some teammates seem uncomfortable around me, or at least I sense they do. Everyone is pleasant enough, but it is their pleasantries that are out of place. Only my closest friends: Lorrei, Scully, Amy, Angie and Cara, treat me the same, with teasing and inside jokes. I miss being one of the girls; I miss being just Haley. Not "Haley Scott, Notre Dame Swimmer." As much pride as I take in that title—the one so many know on the surface—it is those who know me below the surface who make me feel the most comfortable. It is to this I have longed to return.

After my workout we have a long team meeting. We vote for next year's team captains. It seems strange to think about next season; I am so immersed in today.

But the bulk of the meeting involves Assistant Athletic Director Missy Conboy and Bill Kirk, from Student Affairs, discussing the logistics of the accident and our legal options. Notre Dame is doing its best to be open and honest, thorough and helpful. While I respect both Missy and Bill, I barely listen to what they say. I know my situation is different than everyone else's and I know my dad will take care of any legal issues. Instead, my mind wanders as it usually does. I think about one of the times Missy visited me in the hospital, and I smile to myself. It was her birthday and I am still embarrassed about what I said.

"How old are you, 40?" I asked.

She laughed and graciously told me she was only 32. Oops!

Thankfully Missy understood that I am only 18 and under stress and medication. She also looks nowhere near age 40. As Regis Philbin once mentioned on his show, when Missy was in his audience, she might just be "the prettiest Assistant Athletic Director in the NCAA." But when I turn 32, I know I will get a phone call from Missy. And I do. It becomes a running joke between us for years.

Later that night, I head to the library in my golf cart to do a little school work, but mostly to talk. If you want to study seriously, you go to one of the upper levels of the 13-story library. But tonight, Lorrei and I are here as much to socialize as to study, so we are on the notoriously social second floor. A guy named Matt comes over to our table. I think Lorrei has a class with him. Meghan did too.

For the next 20 minutes, Lorrei and I listen as Matt tells us how the accident has affected his life. About how much he misses Meghan, his classmate in a 200-person lecture. About how he is not able to focus on school work, how his grades are failing and how he has been in counseling because he is so devastated by this loss.

Lorrei and I do not know what to say. We will later learn that this is common surrounding tragedy. Many people want to be a part of the tragedy, and to share in the pain, to help lessen it for those who are truly hurting. And I believe Matt, in his own way, is truly hurting. But to Lorrei and me, two 18-year-old girls who are battling emotions we have yet to understand, it is hard to listen to an "outsider." Unknowingly, we have bonded, clicked, or perhaps become a clique. We are swimmers. We are the swim team and we are healing. Don't you dare try to tell me you know how I feel. You don't. Don't you dare tell me how much you understand my loss. You don't. And please do not try to tell me that you know what I am going through, because you don't. Any way you phrase it, you don't.

We are angry. We are hurting and we do not have the energy to think of anyone beyond ourselves, our teammates and our families, usually in that order. This is a time of selfish introspection that, in time, will cease. But for now, you do not understand.

Lorrei and I leave the library annoyed and upset. Outside, however, we cannot find my golf cart. Where did I park it? My memory rivals my menopausal mother's. I am more distracted than ever these days, so I walk around for a minute while Lorrei stands and stares. Once we realize someone has taken it, we burst out laughing. Lorrei doubles over laughing, and I would too, if it weren't for my darn brace.

"Oh my God! I can't believe someone actually took Number Two!" Lorrei says through her laughter.

On another day this might stress me out, but it is one of the best things that could have happened. Lorrei and I cannot stop laughing, and we need a reason to laugh, a reason to smile. Lorrei and I bring Meghan in on the joke; we know if she were here, it would have been she who had taken it.

I call campus security and they drive me across campus to my dorm. Along the way, we find the golf cart at the infirmary. I don't know if I would go so far as to say I hope it happens again, but the comic relief is priceless and needed.

Inside Lyons Hall I visit Amy and Angie to tell them the story of my stolen cart. After a good laugh, Angie and I decide to head down to the Grotto to honor the two-month anniversary of the bus accident. I wonder if I will ever see the date "24th" and not think of the accident. I wonder if I will ever get to the point where I honor only the yearly anniversary. No way, I think. The 24th is too significant.

I love the Grotto, especially at night. Built in 1896, the Grotto is a one-seventh replica of the site in Lourdes, France, where the Virgin Mother reportedly appeared to a young girl, Bernadette. The Grotto on Notre Dame's campus, situated behind Sacred Heart Basilica and across from St. Mary's Lake, is often referred to as the "Cave of Candles." Students, alumni, or anyone can visit, light a candle and say a prayer. Or just sit and think. Or just be in the peaceful glow of the candles. It is a quiet place of reflection. I am sad, but it feels good to be here where I feel so close to Meghan and Colleen. It is cold, but I am warm in the presence of the flames that flicker before me. I stare at the candles as I sit on a bench, then move closer to the kneelers in front. I pray, I cry, but mostly I talk to Meghan and Colleen. I thank them for being with me, for helping me each day and I ask them for their continued guidance. I feel such a presence and so at peace here.

Angie and I move to the grass where we sit and talk for about an hour. We laugh quietly at stories about Colleen and Meghan and reflect upon what happened the night of the accident. The more I relive it, the more it helps. The more I hear what others went through that night, the more I am able to piece together my own memory. As grateful as I am for the medical success of my recovery, I am equally as thankful for the understanding of my teammates for my need to sort through the emotional healing. I am learning I have a long way to go.

Later that week, the swim team attends an auction to raise money for the scholarships founded in Meghan's and Colleen's names. Lou Holtz, our charismatic football coach, "sells" for $25,000 to two people who each bid $12,500.

Overwhelmed by the generosity shown for the memory of my teammates, I turn my head and cry to myself. The women's swim team buys the men's soccer team, and the women's swim team is bought by Rudy Ruettiger. Yes, "Rudy, from the movie *Rudy*," as he will introduce himself to me in the future. He works at a local apartment complex and wants to host a pizza party for us.

The auction raises more than $30,000 and once again I am reminded how proud and honored I am to be a part of Notre Dame Swimming. I put on my blue and gold swim parka like a badge of honor and drive Number Two home.

The next day, Friday, my friend Maren visits. She attends the University of Colorado in Boulder and has been a distant lifeline. She was a diver at Xavier where I swam in high school, but we were mostly friends beyond the pool. For the past two months she has called and written each day. Our nightly phone calls are a break and a relief for me.

She listens without trying to understand, and she entertains me with stories from life at a "real college," as she calls it. I enjoy hearing about rush and her sorority, and the fraternity parties she attends. Many days her phone calls are the only ones that make me laugh. Maren is also a literary outlet for me. When I need to vent or express my thoughts and anger, I often write. And if I am not writing in my journal, I am writing to Maren. Pages and pages, often times during class when I cannot focus, but mostly at night when I cannot sleep. My letters to her become a different sort of journal of my emotions. She had come to see me over Valentine's Day weekend, and I am so excited today to show her how much better I am than when she first visited.

She is amazed. As sadly amazed as she was in February when she saw that I really could not walk; on this trip she is joyfully amazed now that I can. Her genuine hug feels good. Not many people will really hug me. Most people are afraid they will hurt me. But they can't—not with my plastic turtle shell protecting me.

After out-patient therapy, Maren and I drive with Angie to the accident site on the Indiana Toll Road. Coming from campus, we have to drive past the site and make a U-turn to get to the other side of the road, just as Trooper Kubsch did that night. Driving by, I see the yellow CAUTION tape used by the police. Someone has collected the remains of the tape and woven it into the chain-link fence that sits back from the road and runs along the accident site. It reads, "GOD BLESS ND SWIM." I had heard this was here, but it is powerful to actually see it. We turn around and pull over to get out of the car. Up ahead, just 20 or 30 feet, I see a steep ravine. "Wow," I think, "We were really lucky we didn't end up there." I am beginning to take note of the small blessings that will add up to the miracle of my life.

For several minutes Maren, Angie and I walk around in silence. I am not sure Maren knows what to say, but I barely notice. I am trying to piece together what I see in the ground now that the snow has melted: the wheel marks and broken glass. I look around and wonder where they were, where we all were, lying in the snow. It is eerie and it chills me like a gust of wind. For the first time I have intense flashbacks of that night. I remember details that never before crossed my mind: passing the pizza boxes forward after skipping on that last piece of pizza; the sound of Meghan laughing, so full of life, when she talked to Shana; how sitting next to Colleen made me feel better about the world, about myself. There was such hope on that bus. Now, at the site, all that remains is the cold ground, muddied with tire marks and half-damp green grass.

There is the cement block, a culvert, about 18-inches wide. Is this what we hit? Is this the culvert that catapulted our bus to flip upside down? I am stunned. It is buried, barely visible above the grass, yet the bus managed to hit it. For the first time I realize what a truly freak accident it was. Just inches either way and everyone's lives would be different, perhaps saved.

Standing on the incline off the side of the road, I once again feel the bus skidding and my loss of equilibrium. I grab Angie's arm to steady myself, even though I am not really falling. Or am I? I am dizzy with the memory of that night, spinning with the intense force of the flip of a bus. I am on my back in the snow with Scully next to me. I close my eyes and see Lorrei standing over me with the same dazed look I saw when she visited me in the hospital. It is a beautiful day, but all I can see is the snow blowing and the dark confusion of that night. I squint in the sunlight to look at where so many lives were left in shambles; at this very spot where lives changed, and ended.

Still holding on, I bend down to collect some glass and a bright yellow headset from a SONY Walkman. Is this mine? Is it Meghan's? We each owned one. Or is it someone else's? I have no idea, but I scoop the headset up, hold it to my chest and say a quick prayer, because to whomever it belonged, we all need prayers.

So much tragedy surrounds this accident. The swimmers, our families and the Notre Dame community are all affected to various degrees. It is hard to explain to people that Meghan and Colleen were once-in-a-lifetime people, not only to their families, but also to us. What I do not yet realize in my isolated world of healing is that everyone is unique, with special talents and gifts; it is just that Meghan and Colleen are personal to me. They are the faces of my tragedy.

I recall watching the video of Father Malloy's homily from the Memorial Mass that January afternoon. "Our swimmers are no longer children," he said. I did not understand his words at the time, but he is right; we are not. That too is part of the tragedy. We never viewed ourselves as children, but now there is no going back. I am beginning to understand our loss of innocence.

As we walk back up to the car, I pause at two roses stuck in the ground. I am told they are always here—a marker of beauty at the scene of tragedy. They remind those who drive by of all we are trying to forget. Yet they symbolize and honor the lives of our friends. I tell Meghan and Colleen good-bye and feel as though there is one less missing piece in the puzzle that is my life.

At the end of the weekend when Maren has left, I call my parents. I have not spoken to them since Maren's arrival three days ago, and my mother asks question after question about everything. She wants to know every detail: how I am feeling, the details of therapy and of how all my friends are doing. For eight weeks she shared our world—mine and everyone else's. Now, she knows little more than what I tell her in a 15-minute daily—or in this case, twice weekly— phone call. Despite my annoyance at the abundance of questions she asks, or perhaps because of it, I realize I can no longer skip a day of calling. Like the rest of us, my mom is trying to deal with her own emotions.

My mother is unhappy and I feel badly for her. She is desperate to be here, but she knows she cannot be. I do not want her here and she knows it is not "normal" for her to be here. What freshman in college has their mother living at the hotel on campus? I know she wants me to have as normal a life as possible, but she also knows that my life is not normal. Despite her inner desire to be with me, and to do whatever she can to make my life easier, my mother understands there is a lot I am going to have to experience and come to terms with on my own. But that is not easy for a mother who has just watched her child struggle and suffer and who desperately wants to protect her daughter from more pain.

I think I overdid it today. I had a Spanish test in the morning, which went pretty well. And then I had therapy at noon, which I know is good for me, but it is also a reminder that I am not well, not "normal." Whatever "normal" is, I just wish it would return. Back on campus I lifted weights: triceps, biceps and some leg exercises. Then came the best part: getting in the pool. I kicked and swam with fins, and went my farthest distance yet: 2,400 yards. Class, an exam, therapy, lifting weights and swimming—I definitely overdid it. Lying in bed, my back aches, my legs tingle, and I hurt too much to fall asleep. I am annoyed at myself for doing too much and annoyed at my body for not being able to handle it. Yet, I know I need to be grateful that my body can do anything at all. And I am. I really am. It is a paradox I live with daily.

Tonight I worry and wonder if I am going to have to relearn how to swim. Of course I can swim, but I mean swim like a swimmer—a collegiate swimmer. I can get in the water and do the strokes, but it is not the same. I am tired of relearning old things; I am tired of learning new things, for that matter. Still, the same questions linger in my mind: Will I ever be as good a swimmer as I once was? How long will that take? I want so desperately to swim again, but I also want to swim fast. I want to be the swimmer I was before, maybe better.

I do not consider myself a fearful person, but I am so afraid of failure. And failure now means not being 100 percent again. I also know most people do not understand this. Perhaps my perception is distorted and impractical. Maybe I am being selfish, or unrealistic, but I do not know if I want to compete again if I cannot be as good as I was before. But I will be; I have to be, no matter how long it takes. There is no other option for me. I am that determined. Plus, I owe it to Meghan and Colleen. I promised them I would walk and swim again for them. They helped me achieve one goal and I am sure with their help, competing again is a feat my body will deliver. I know I will get up on the starting blocks and swim the 100-yard butterfly for Colleen and the 50-yard freestyle for Meghan. They will be so proud of me. For them, I would do anything. And with them, I will. It is the best way I know to honor their memory.

At times I sense an unwelcome stranger overtake me. Hate. I hate the accident, I hate buses and I hate United Limo—the bus company. I hate death. I hate being tired and in pain all the time. I hate wearing this brace. I hate having to be nice when I don't feel nice inside. I want to love life again, to love swimming, to love whatever the future holds for me. But I do not know what the future holds, and that makes me fearful. I hate fear. This cannot be healthy. I get angry when these feelings overcome me. Sometimes the littlest things set me off and send me into a bad mood. It is nothing specific that anyone has done, I just hate what has happened, and anything else just adds to the frustration. It also does not help that I have no one I feel comfortable getting mad at when my mom is not here. She is my emotional punching bag. But in her absence, I am forced to internalize this anger and it wears me down. I love Notre Dame, yet I am ready to go home for the summer. Without schoolwork, I will have nothing to deal with except physical and emotional healing. Maybe I should drop my math class.

After a restless weekend of aching legs and little sleep, I attend only one of three classes on Monday. I do not have the energy to do more. I keep rereading the article from Sunday's *South Bend Tribune*. It is really good and makes me cry; but these days, that does not take much. The reporter, Patti Auer, did a thorough job of researching and interviewing everyone from my doctors to my therapists to my mother. It presents a comprehensive overview of the last two months of my life. One comment, though, surprises me: one doctor states that he does not know if "Haley will ever recover to where she needs to be to compete at the level she was at." They might not know, but I know. And so do Colleen and Meghan. I will swim again for Notre Dame.

I guarantee it.

The date is April 8, and I am going to see Meghan today. I am excited to visit her, but cannot explain it in a context that would make sense to anyone, not even myself. I know I need to go and I know I want to go, but I am nervous with anticipation.

I sit with Meghan for 90 minutes. I tell her stories from the team and update her on how everyone is healing from, and dealing with, the accident. And then I wonder: How would Meghan deal with the accident right now? Would she latch onto the deceased's families? Would she try to ignore it happened by surrounding herself with non-swimmer friends? Would she spend time with only swimmers and immerse herself in the grief of the accident? Or would she retreat into her own private world and study how it has affected and changed her life? All of these varied options are taking place within our team. One is not right and one is not wrong. We are all trying to heal the best we know how.

Mostly, I sit quietly and alternate between looking at Meghan's grave and looking up to see the Golden Dome. I thank Meghan and Colleen for watching over me and for helping me walk. Again, I make a promise to compete. I believe they have been a part of this; I know they have. And I believe they continue to look after me, even though they have so many other people to whom they give their spirit, especially their parents and siblings, whose sense of loss must dwarf my own.

As I talk to them, a guy skates up on rollerblades. He slows down when he sees me, when he sees that Meghan is not alone.

"Are you Haley?" he asks quietly, afraid that he has interrupted my time here.

"Yes," I answer, with as much of a smile as I can muster.

"How are you doing?"

I am not able to answer this question, and he quickly realizes it. Maybe he sees the dampness on my cheeks from tears cried, or the new ones in my eyes. I nod my head, both to indicate that I am doing well and that I am unable to speak. He looks down, almost embarrassed, and apologizes as he rolls away. I try to speak, but the tears still choke me. I wish I could tell him it is okay, that I am okay, and that he should not feel sorry for me. But I am also glad he left. I do not want to talk to anyone else right now. I know I am being selfish in wanting to be alone at Meghan's grave. I hope for her sake that he returns, so she is left alone as little as possible.

I really need to come here more often. It is almost like the Grotto for me; it is a sacred place where I feel close to my friends. It is not like I do not think about Meghan and Colleen every day. How could I not? Each ache of my back is a reminder. Each trip on my golf cart is a reminder. Each time I see a United Limo bus on campus, I am reminded. I am not sure how it started, but every time I see those blue, white and gray buses, I stop my thoughts and say an entire "Hail Mary" to myself. Why? I do not know. In honor and respect, I guess. I do this until I graduate.

"Why?" is a question I have been asking myself lately. I do not tell anyone else, and I often deny it when people ask, "Do you ever wonder why this happened?" No. My "whys" are private, more of a demand than a question. "Why! Why on Earth did this happen?" Well, I guess that is the answer. It did not happen on Earth. It was God who made the decision and it is our team who has to deal with it. And why am I all right? Why was I hurt, yet I am still alive? There has to be some reason, some purpose to my—to our—suffering. What is our destiny and why must we endure this suffering to prepare for it?

14

Our team banquet is today. The end of the season. The end of two lives. What are we celebrating?

That is my hurt and my anger talking. The team has a lot to celebrate: finishing the season, uniting in our grief, and healing together. We have risen to meet this challenge, and we have beaten the odds because we are a team. My teammates look to me for hope. I am the tangible healing they feel inside. It is only I who does not feel this. I had other wounds to heal first. But today the team celebrates how far we have come since January 24th.

The coaches and captains institute a new award this year: the Beeler-Hipp Award. This award honors the freshman who best exemplifies the love and spirit shown by Meghan and Colleen during their first year at Notre Dame. Finding someone who represents the best of these two girls will be difficult; they were both good people, but in such different ways.

Meghan was a straight-A blonde who danced on tables and was the life of the party, often a rare combination.

Colleen was quiet, positive and never complained as she worked her hardest to swim well and fulfill her ROTC obligations. Meghan made plans to go out and organized our social life, while Colleen made cassette tape music mixes and organized our holiday accessories. There are qualities in each of them to which I aspire, but to encompass both personalities would be difficult. The coaches, not surprisingly, get it right when they chose to honor them with the two things they did have in common: swimming and their love for Notre Dame. But we all share that. How do we honor one of us over the other? I think the award should go to the entire freshman class, but if I had to vote, I would vote for Lorrei. She knew them both the best.

This year's recipient will be unique because she will have known Meghan and Colleen and will be honored in her friends' names. The swimmers who receive this award in the future will know it to be just that: an award. But to us, the team of the 1991-92 season, this award is personal.

At the banquet that morning at Tippecanoe Place, the Beeler-Hipp Award is bestowed upon me. I am humbled and honored. Meghan and Colleen were my friends, my teammates. I am so proud of this award and to be associated with them. Our names are now forever linked; me and these two girls who I will always call my friends. I cannot explain the feeling, yet I cannot remember ever being so deeply touched. I will do all I can to live up to this award and prove I am worthy of being honored in Meghan's and Colleen's names.

I look at the calendar: April 14. Today, I meet with Dr. Keucher at Memorial Hospital. My energy level and moods dwindle as the semester winds down, and my emotional well-being hinges on some good news today.

Dr. Keucher has nothing of the sort.

After an examination and a full set of X-rays, he determines that I am not healed enough to take off my brace. In fact, it might be several months before I am ready to walk brace-free. With my spine continuing to collapse and angle forward, Dr. Keucher confirms I will need to have surgery to straighten my spine. Not "in the future," which I thought meant years, but this summer. I am afraid and I panic.

When I return to my dorm, Sister Kathleen recognizes the fear in my eyes, my body language, and my slightly stooped posture. She knows something is terribly wrong. She knows what I have denied to myself for weeks, but in my heart I knew was true: that my back is not healing as fast as I had hoped it would. In fact, it is not healing at all. It is getting worse. I should know this because the pain is constant. Sister K gives me a hug. It is nice to have a motherly hug. I miss my mom. But right now I want to be alone. Sister Kathleen walks me silently to my room, just two doors down from her own.

Fortunately for me, my father has been dealing with the accident in the best way he knows how. He has been searching nationally for the best back surgeon for his daughter. He finds Dr. Steven Garfin, an orthopedic specialist at the University of California—San Diego Medical Center. Dr. Garfin specializes in the rare type of surgery I require. He performs 10-12 of these operations a year, which is considered a lot. My dad sends Dr. Garfin a case summary and the X-rays of my back that were taken the day I left the hospital in March.

It is Easter weekend and most people have gone home. My dad and my brother come for the holiday so I do not have to travel. My mom stays home to be with Mary Frances and to drive her to a volleyball tournament in Santa Barbara with my grandmother. I know my mom wants to be here too, but I also know she needs to be with my sister right now.

"Stephen!" I yell when I see him. If I could run to give him a hug, I would. I am thrilled to see him and excited to show him how well I can walk. He has not seen me since one week after the accident. I still walk slowly, sometimes with a cane, and each step is calculated. But I am walking. One day I hope to stand up and walk without thinking about it, but for now I am happy just to walk unaided.

As my brother and I smile, laugh and enjoy this reunion, my dad watches solemnly. It is obvious that he is having a hard time. He tells me he can barely work, that all he does is think about what has happened and what I have been through. But it is more than that. He knows my back hurts and aches all the time, and he cannot stand the thought of my being in constant pain.

It devastates him to see his daughter pretend she is okay, and I know he would do anything to take away the pain. He hates to leave me in my dorm at night because he knows I have trouble sleeping. He wants to do everything possible to make my life easier. For his sake, I wish there was something he could do to help me. I can deal with my life; I am managing and I will continue to manage. I have a huge support group here. But my dad … he is so upset, and feeling so helpless. I spend the weekend trying to ease his worries, but with little success.

My dad does not want to leave at the end of the weekend. I can tell by his hesitation. He, who is always in control and anxious to get to the airport early, does not want to give up a minute of time with me. "How can we leave her here?" He begs to my mom on the phone from the airport. My dad is finally beginning to understand the desperation my mom has felt for weeks.

Lying in bed, the song 'End of the Innocence' comes on. I love this song, but it makes me cry. I have never been so emotional in my life. I feel as though I am reaching the end. I need a break from my life.

Two more weeks until I go home. One week of classes, one week of finals and my mom comes in eight days—yeah! I cannot wait to see her. But first, this weekend is Pig Tostal, a variation of An Tostal, Notre Dame's spring celebration. An Tostal began in Ireland in 1953, with parades, art festivals and sporting events designed to celebrate Celtic culture and attract tourists at Easter time. For Pig Tostal, swimmers parade around the Swim House wearing t-shirts of original artwork and participating in a different sort of sport. Our efforts attract our own tourists, or non-swimmers, to this annual festival featuring bands and a pig roast.

The day of Pig Tostal is cold and rainy. I wear my swim parka, and several teammates take turns sitting with me as we enjoy people watching. I know, like everyone else celebrating spring, that we have a long week of studying and finals ahead of us. We are all thankful for the diversion.

Finals week is a struggle and an emotional roller coaster that mirrors my semester. I can barely focus for more than a few minutes. Studying Calculus and conjugating Spanish verbs seem so trivial when I am trying to figure out how to live in this body. My education this semester cannot be found in a textbook, and I have a hard time focusing on anything that is. But I still stress about my grades. I want to do well enough to pass so I do not have to retake these classes.

On Monday night, I am the keynote speaker at the Michiana Nurses Appreciation Dinner. I spend more time writing and rewriting my speech than studying for any exam I take this week, a clear indication of my priorities and where my mind is. But I really want to do a good job conveying how much I appreciate my nurses' skills, care and concern for both me and my family. The doctors may have worked on my back, but the nurses took care of me day after day.

"Great nurses make all the difference," I tell them. I receive a standing ovation.

The next day I am exhausted and decide to drop Calculus. I only have the final left to take, but I just cannot do it. I have an English paper to write and a Spanish exam for which to study. Math, once my favorite subject, just is not going to happen. I tried as best I could, but I am exhausted and stressed. Thank goodness Dr. Wong gave me this option. My parents are thrilled. To them, my job is to take care of myself and to rest. School is secondary.

My mom is here, and I will be home in four days. Not that I am counting.

The night before we return to Phoenix, I stay up until 4 a.m. with my freshmen teammates. We have become a unique group because of all we have gone through over the past four months. As the hours pass late into the night, we talk and cry, celebrate and remember a time that we are ready to leave, a semester we are ready to end. Yet I cannot believe we will not see each other for three months. I need them, yet I also need to go home. We all do. I can sense that Lorrei is ready to leave too. She carries a heavy burden: to be my friend, to make me laugh and to stay positive for me, all while internalizing her own grief. She was the humor and the strength that got me through my hospital stay. But she needs the summer to take care of herself and to get away from her own daily reminders of the accident.

Angie and I make one last late-night trip to the Grotto. We stay longer than we had planned, talking about the summer and of course about Meghan and Colleen, and what they might have done over the summer. We laugh some, but there is a quiet sadness between us. Angie will return to campus in June. She is retaking control of her future by taking classes and getting ahead in her Business major. But my summer plans are unknown. I know I will have surgery, but I am too scared to think or talk about it. I am afraid of being away from my teammates and away from Notre Dame.

15

May 12, 1992

Not long after I am home in Phoenix, Dr. Garfin calls. More bad news. More puzzle pieces of my complicated life are not fitting together.

"Haley needs to get off her feet immediately," he says. "Her spine is collapsed. The rods have broken away from her vertebrae and are not providing any support."

What? The X-rays are from March; it is now May. I have been walking around with a collapsed spine for two months. The rods are no longer attached to my spine? How did that happen and why did we not know? The only thing providing support is my turtle shell brace. I am instructed to lie down as much as possible and to prepare for surgery in June. But first I need to meet this doctor, for my sake and for my parents' sake.

We fly to San Diego to meet with Dr. Garfin. The flight is short, but still painful and uncomfortable for me. My Aunt Barbara and my cousin Tracey, a sophomore at the University of San Diego, join us at the doctor's office.

Dr. Steven Garfin is great. He is young, friendly, very direct and confident that he is the best person to perform the operation. That is what I want. His confidence is comforting. As Dr. Garfin explains the surgery in three parts, we rely on his confidence even more.

The first task is to remove the broken, unattached Cotrell-Dubousset instrumentation (the rods used in the South Bend surgery) and clean out the partial fusion. The last part will be to attach Edwards instrumentation (new rods) in my back. The middle part is the trickiest, the longest and the most dangerous. As Dr. Garfin explains, imagine a tree. My spine, he states, is like a tree that is bent over. In South Bend, the doctors tried to pull the tree straight from behind. The better way to do it is to go in from the front, get more leverage, and push the spine up. This makes sense to me. I can picture it and I get it.

The middle task is complicated and cutting edge, so to speak. To minimize problems, Dr. Garfin will have a trauma surgeon, Dr. Robert Winchell, do the actual entry to my spine. Dr Garfin likes to use a trauma surgeon in difficult surgeries, because in his opinion they are good to have in the operating room if things go wrong. Dr. Winchell—or Dr. Donut, as we fondly call him, since Winchell's Donuts were my favorite pre-meet breakfast when I was in middle school—will open and close the "anterior" or frontal approach. He will open up my body to allow Dr. Garfin to reach the front of my collapsed spine. Dr. Donut will lay me on my side and his cut will extend from my right shoulder blade, curling around under my arm and halfway across my chest.

"We will have to remove a rib, maybe two, deflate a lung and move organs out of the way." Dr. Garfin speaks matter-of-factly. I hear him and try to digest it matter-of-factly. There are times, usually in public, when I have a unique ability to distance myself from what is happening to my body. Move organs? Like my stomach? And tying off an artery that carries blood to my heart? My dad stands to my right with his yellow legal pad, writing everything down. My mom is on my left listening, and wondering how we can choose to do this. For her, South Bend was easier; the surgery was done before she got there.

My mom hears the term "myelogram," a test I will need to have, and she gets a headache. She had a myelogram before her own back surgery and it was horrible. Her memory of the large needle and the pain prevents her from hearing little else. My cousin Tracey feels faint and leaves the room as Dr. Garfin continues to describe in detail the operation and its potential complications. One by one my support network checks out. I hope this is not an indication of what surgery will be like in San Diego.

Dr. Garfin continues.

"Any re-operation is technically harder because of scar tissue, because one has to separate scar tissue from the neural elements, or the spinal cord, and from the previous bone. Right now you have a partial fusion which has to be taken down (the graft from my hip done in South Bend) and you have part of your tenth rib removed. The ideal rib to remove to allow access to the spinal cord would have been the eighth or the ninth. However, I will remove all of your tenth rib to avoid taking down more ribs. So our approach will be somewhat compromised by what has already been done in South Bend."

Thank goodness my dad is writing this down.

"To further compound the situation, it has been four months since your other operations. There is pressure on the spinal cord, plus scar tissue, plus recurring deformity and one doesn't know prognostically what that means to the spinal cord in terms of the ability to recover from another insult. Another insult being surgery and anesthesia, which in itself, is trauma to the spinal cord.

"The key is getting a good fit for the bone graft in the front of your spine so it will be straight again. It is your choice whether we harvest your femur bone or use a cadaver donor bone. After the bone graft is held in place with a metal plate, this second part of the operation is closed up," Dr. Garfin says.

To support this new anterior bone graft, Dr. Garfin has to do basically another operation. He will enter again through the incision on my back to install, what he describes as "big, heavy, metal rods and hooks and bone from your pelvis to fuse the spine. We will have to do that in the same area that was previously operated on, which is not easy, because of the abundance of scar tissue.

"It is a difficult surgery, both for the patient and the surgeon, but far more for the patient. It wears you out with no guarantee. There is a chance you could come out of it worse. You might come out with the same kyphosis, but a little less pain. But the hope is that you will be better, maybe even a lot better."

Dr. Garfin pauses and looks me straight in the eye. "Haley, this is a very fatiguing surgery. It is like getting hit by a Mack truck. You will be exhausted and you will be expected to stay on your back for six to eight weeks. No sitting and minimal walking. After open heart surgery, this is the second most difficult operation for a patient. You are young and strong, so you will be able to fight through and heal. But you don't want to go through it twice.

"Heart surgery," Garfin explains, "is a life or death issue. You have it or you die. With this surgery we are talking quality of life and function. You may die or you may be paralyzed, and there is always risk of infection…"

My focus fades as I try to listen and comprehend everything Dr. Garfin is saying: it is fatiguing, because it is stage after stage of surgery; the recovery period is long, because all of my insides will have to heal. It is a delicate and difficult procedure. Move my heart. Move my lungs. Move the vessels that go from my heart to the rest of my body. Once again, I try to separate myself from my body as I realize every major organ will be at risk with this operation.

I too feel faint and take a noticeably deep breath.

Dr. Garfin pauses when he sees the grim looks on our faces.

"But I can do it," he says. "And I am confident that I can get you the best results possible."

He pauses again to let this bit of reassurance sink in. Yet he knows he has to be realistic.

"A collapsed spine is not good. I would rather have operated on you when you were first injured, than to try to go back in and fix something that someone else has already tried to fix."

Dr. Garfin is aware that this is not going to be easy.

On the way home, my father assures me that Dr. Garfin is the very best in the country for this type of surgery.

I carry no resentment toward the medical care I received in South Bend, but I suspect my father does. In my mind, Dr. Keucher saved my legs. He is a neurosurgeon and he saved my nerves as best he could. Now my spine needs to be fixed properly, and that requires someone with Dr. Garfin's experience and expertise.

While there is apprehension about the nature of my upcoming surgery, there is also a tangible feeling of relief that Dr. Garfin is now my surgeon.

I spend the next three weeks in Phoenix, doing little more than watching *The Young & the Restless*, chatting with visitors and donating blood once a week. I will lose a lot of blood during surgery and the more of my own they use to replenish, the better. But it takes a toll. The first time I donate I am fine, until I eat my cookie and juice and stand up to leave. Then I faint. The next week, I faint as I am getting up from the reclined donation chair. The final week, I faint as they are still drawing blood. Taking three units of blood in as many weeks from a healthy person would be a lot. But for my worn down body and equally trodden soul, it is too much. I am coming to the end of my tolerance. I have had enough. Enough pain, enough sadness and enough idleness. It has to get better than this.

Susan Taylor, a journalist with the local CBS affiliate who specializes in medical stories, comes to do a preoperative interview. It will air in Phoenix over Memorial Day weekend, before my surgery in San Diego. The difference between Ms. Taylor's interview now and the one I gave over Spring Break could not contrast more. As upbeat and optimistic as I was in March, I am more frightened and weary now. The difference is remarkable. And in two months when she comes to visit me in San Diego, it is that much worse.

It is May 28 and surgery is scheduled for June 2. Still off my feet, Dr. Tabor, a local orthopedic doctor, has prescribed two different antibiotics for an oozing sore on my back. What my mom first noticed in March as a small bruise has slowly deteriorated; first oozing a clear, yellowish discharge and now leaking a brown and cloudy goo. An infection at this time would complicate an already complicated surgery. As the pain in my back intensifies, my body aches from fatigue and my roller coaster emotions leave me equally exhausted.

It is hard to be so tired all the time. I feel like I am in limbo, waiting for the next phase of my life. I have nothing to look forward to, nothing to plan, nothing to talk or laugh about, and no good friends around who understand me. It is fun to have old high school friends visit and tell me stories from their own lives at college. But they have not lived the last few months with me. As sad as they might have been when they first heard about the accident, it does not consume their lives. And as sorry as they may feel for me when they visit today, they will still go out tonight and have fun. I am grateful for their time and I appreciate their efforts to see me, but we have little left in common except our high school diplomas. My life is too different and theirs have moved on. As they should. But that is hard for me.

I find little to comfort me: Nancy's daily visits, mail, phone calls from my teammates and watching television with my dad. *Jeopardy!*

and *Wheel of Fortune* entertain us each night. Dad and I play against each other, seeing who can shout out answers first. I usually win, but maybe he lets me.

Tonight as I lay on my stomach, my mother takes off the back part of my brace to change my t-shirt and apply a clean dressing over the bruise.

I ask my nightly question:

"How does it look?"

What she sees sends waves of fear and panic through her body. Yet, she answers the way she always does: calmly, positively, and as honestly as she can.

"Well…" she pauses, "there is a little blood."

16

Looking back, I realize, "a little blood" was an understatement. There was a lot of blood. My undershirt and the bandage covering my wound were soaked with blood. "A little blood." What was my mom thinking with that description? She wasn't. She was trying to protect me from her fear and from the horror she saw on my back and felt in her heart.

It was my rods. The small bruise, that the doctors in South Bend told us resulted from my brace pressing on my bone chip, was in fact caused by my unattached rods. As my unsupported back had increasingly angled forward, one rod detached from the vertebrae it was supposed to be supporting and broke through my skin, leaving an open wound about a centimeter long. Thank God I had no feeling on the surface of my back. While my muscles ached and the bone pain caused daily suffering, the nerve endings of the skin were numb, if not from my injury, then from the surgeon's knife. Either way, those dead nerve endings were a blessing.

With this new complication, Dr. Garfin insisted I come to San Diego immediately. This frightened me. Why did he feel the need to move up my surgery three days? It scared me to think that it might be that serious; that just three days might make a difference. That Dr. Garfin was willing to operate on a holiday weekend because of a little infection. It was that serious.

My dad drove to California early the next morning, in time to pick up my mom and me at San Diego International Airport after our quick 45-minute flight. We headed straight toward the University of California—San Diego (UCSD) Medical Center, my home for the next three weeks. If I had known how bad the next three weeks would be, I would have been more scared. But again, my mother's positive energy was calming.

I was admitted on the Friday of Memorial Day weekend with normal vital signs, but a low-grade fever. This indicated a possible infection. The next morning I underwent emergency surgery to avoid further risk of "contamination," as Dr. Garfin described it. During the two-hour operation, Dr. Garfin, assisted by Dr. Blair and a U.S. Navy officer, Dr. Green, removed the Cotrell-Dubousset instrumentation. In less than two hours the rods came out, and were later found to have no defects, according to the pathology report. Nothing was wrong with the rods themselves; they just did not fit well in my broken back.

The surgery also answered some questions and raised some new ones. In this surgery, Dr. Garfin noted I have a pediatric skeleton. Technically an adult at 18, I still had children's bones, bones more malleable and less brittle than a fully developed 18-year-old's bones. It was an inherited blessing; a gift from my deceased grandmother. It had been discussed in our initial visit at Dr. Garfin's office whether to use my own bone or a cadaver's bone for my definitive anterior bone graft. With the discovery of my small skeleton, a cadaver bone it would be, a pediatric cadaver. A four-inch long, weight-bearing child's leg bone would be used. Another family's grief was another gift to me, and another angel to watch over me along with Meghan and Colleen.

The surgery also allowed Dr. Garfin to explore my spine, to assess the damage and to determine the best course of action. Because of this first-hand knowledge, the myelogram test that had given my mother a headache was not needed. Dr. Garfin was able to see more during surgery than any test or X-ray could show. Thank goodness. No test and no more needles.

However, the straightforward rod removal operation did not come without its own headaches. After surgery, I was wheeled back to my room on my new Rotobed. This bed was exactly like it sounds.

I looked like a blue Gumby. Because my spine was not support-ed by rods or a brace, I was unable to do anything but lie flat on my back and remain completely still. But lying flat can cause pressure sores. So this bed was equipped with panels down each side of my arms, legs, head and torso, with straps crisscrossing my body to hold me in place while the bed rotated from side to side. I was told the bed rotated at a speed slower than the human body can detect so I would not feel as though I was tilting. Not so. While the slowly moving bed might have fooled my inner ear, it did not fool gravity. Each time I rotated to one side, I felt my body ever-so-gently shift to that side. It was annoying, and never-ending. Back and forth, back and forth. For what turned out to be almost two weeks.

The three days between surgeries alternated between boring and humorous. I felt well, was not in too much pain—thanks to my PCA pump—and was fully alert while waiting for my next operation. The Rotobed was still a novelty and the bilateral venodynes (inflating and deflating wraps on my legs to prevent a blood clot) felt like a little leg massage. All my tests and levels of whatever they were monitoring fell within normal ranges, although I did begin to show signs of anemia. Television was difficult to watch from a flat position with my head held in place by a halo. So I limited myself to *The Young and the Restless*, and my mom began reading to me. Whenever I had to go to the bathroom, which with a constant IV and my nerve-damaged bladder was all the time, my mom would ring the nurse.

"I have no idea how to operate this bed," each nurse replied during the different shifts. The Rotobed was rarely seen outside the Intensive Care Unit, so these nurses were not familiar with this new technology. Thank goodness my mom had been there when the technician explained the bed, because nurse or no nurse, I still had to go to the bathroom—and badly. After several attempts to explain the bed to the nurses, my mom would read my face and take matters into her own hands. Literally. She would stop the rotation of the bed and hold it steady with one hand while she shoved in a pin to "freeze" the bed. Then, she would crawl on the floor underneath the bed to remove the panel below the appropriate part of my body in order to hold up a bed pan for me to use. It took a few tries to get it right, but eventually she figured out a system and actually got quite good at it. So much for my "high tech" bed in all matters organic. Thank goodness we both still had our sense of humor, however warped it was.

As the weekend came to a close, I prepared for my "major" surgery. The night before, my parents and I met with the anesthesiologist as preoperative protocol. Because the doctors wanted to monitor my body's response during surgery—to test my legs and nerves to make sure there was no additional damage or setbacks occurring as a result of the surgeon's manipulations of my spine—I could not be fully anesthetized. This left me with two options: I could be completely put under anesthesia for most of the surgery and woken during the operation to measure my neurological response; or I could be given a lighter anesthesia, one that would allow my body to respond to stimuli during surgery. Both options came with red flags. The first type of anesthesia would require a longer operation time, with time enough to wake me up and put me back under. The latter would allow the doctors to proceed in a timelier manner, but I was told I might hear voices and sounds from the operating room throughout the surgery.

What? What kind of choices were those? A longer operation or hearing voices while they operated but not being able to talk or move? I do not know why or what my reasoning, but I chose the latter. I had already gone under, and come out of, anesthesia once that week. That had not been the original plan, and it certainly complicated matters by putting my body through another operation, but with the rods breaking through and the high risk of infection, I was left with no choice. But this was the big one: Dr. Garfin was going to straighten my spine. He could do it because he was the best. He even alluded to that himself.

The day June 2, began early and ended late. In some ways, it did not end for more than a week. But that morning, as I was prepped for surgery: IV lines, deep breaths with a mask on, the cold operating room and the bright lights, all I thought about was what Dr. Garfin said about not wanting to go through this twice. Once was enough.

"You will feel like you've been hit by a Mack truck," he told me. "But you are young and you'll be fine. You just wouldn't want to do it twice."

Never twice. Only once. Not something "your body could go through twice." Okay, got it. Once will be more than enough.

So, once it was. I could do this.

Music. There was music playing in the operating room. I wondered what type of music Dr. Garfin would listen to when he was cutting me open. I had visions of my favorite movie *The Silence of the Lambs* and the loud classical music that played while Dr. Hannibal Lector performed his own type of surgery. I hoped it wasn't that.

"Are you ready?" a nurse asked.

Ready to be hit by a truck, ready to take my body to the edge and pray that youth and Dr. Garfin could pull me back in time to get through it? Yes, I was ready to do it once.

I nodded with a faint smile beneath the mask. The clock read 9:15 a.m.

At 1:30 p.m. an intra-operative report indicated that Dr. Winchell had performed a right thoracotomy (an incision into the chest cavity) for his anterior approach, and that Dr. Garfin and his team were performing the orthopedic portion of the surgery. This included: a T-10 corpectomy (removal of the bone at the T-10 level); a partial T-9 and T-11 corpectomy; T8-9 and T11-12 discectomies (removal of the disc); and the anterior fusion of T-8 to T-12 with Edward's instrumentation (more rods). The report also showed that I required "unusually large doses of narcotic medication," and that I had lost a total of 4,900 cc of blood (approximately half of the body's blood volume). My body was in trauma.

3:30 p.m. The surgery did not go well. My parents saw it in Dr. Garfin's body language as soon as he walked out of the operating room. My parents stood up and their anxious faces asked their questions without words.

"Haley is...fine. It went," he paused again and closed his eyes, "all right."

Dr. Garfin was holding something back, and my parents could tell. My father did not accept that kind of answer. He wanted the truth, even if it hurt.

And it did hurt.

"I really did not get the result I wanted. Her back is straighter than it was, but not as upright as I had hoped for. It had been bent for just too long." Dr. Garfin said, disappointed. "She should be better, but there will be chronic pain, and probably arthritis in the back."

The fact that it had healed improperly for four months did not help.

"It was just too broken to straighten completely," he explained helplessly.

What do you say in a moment like that? What words did one use to tell parents that their daughter was just...too broken to be fixed? All the king's horses, all the king's men…Mr. and Mrs. Scott, we could not put your daughter back together again.

"Dr. Winchell is just closing her up," said the once-confident doctor, who was as competitive as his patient and did not like the unfamiliar feeling of defeat. "You should be able to see her in about two hours."

My parents tried to absorb it. They too felt defeated and exhausted, yet they knew Dr. Garfin had done the best he could and was the best there was. And I would be the best I could be because of him. My mom focused on her watch for the next couple of hours, waiting desperately to see me.

Two hours came and went. Then three, and four. My parents stood, sat and paced outside the double doors of the Post-Anesthesia Care Unit (PACU) until they were the only people remaining in the waiting room. My parents were frantic and desperate to see me, desperate to know why they had to wait two hours longer than they were told. What did that mean? Was I okay? Was I alone? Finally, in the deserted island of the waiting room, my parents begged a random doctor to allow them to see me.

Inside the PACU, I remembered little. I had not heard voices or sounds during surgery, or if I had, I did not remember. Thank goodness. But when I woke up and slowly came out of sedation, I panicked. I could not move and I could not breathe. I was still ventilated, which prevented me from breathing on my own. I could not talk and I did not see anyone who looked familiar. My eyes darted back and forth looking for something recognizable. I was scared. Any time a nurse came over I tried to motion that I could not breathe, but each time they told me politely to relax and rest.

Finally, my parents entered the dark room and walked past the only occupied bed. I was so bloated that I was unrecognizable to them. The nurse motioned them back and my mom felt as ill as I looked when she saw me for the first time. My body had been pumped with IV fluids during the surgery to make up for blood loss; I was swollen and appeared to have no ears, no nose and only slits for eyes. My eyes continued to dart back and forth until they finally came to rest on those I knew.

I tried to tell my parents that I could not breathe and my mom rushed to tell the nurse. I won't say the nurse was annoyed, but she came across as less than sympathetic as she explained that the ventilator does not allow the body to breathe on its own. So of course I felt like I could not breathe, but I was getting enough oxygen.

"I explained that to your daughter," she stated.

"Well, my daughter can't talk!" my mother wanted to yell.

But Mom was too tired and too stunned, and did her best to remain focused on me. The nurse explained further that I was too swollen to remove the ventilation tube, for fear of my throat closing. With the amount of blood I lost during surgery, I needed to replenish my fluids. I used up three units of auto-donor blood (my own) and four units of donor-specific A-negative blood (from friends in Phoenix who also had this blood type), in addition to several others, including packed red blood cells from a blood bank. I was given a blood coagulant to prevent additional bleeding, but this required the doctors to stop recycling the blood I lost during surgery. I would later be annoyed that I had suffered through donating my own blood, in an effort to minimize my exposure to strangers' donated blood, since I used banked blood anyway. But the reality was I had bled so much during the operation that I required all the donor blood available.

My parents were usually optimistic and positive when they were with me, so I did not understand their lack of encouraging words. Actually, I didn't really understand much of anything at this time. All I knew was that there was a tube that felt like it was preventing me from breathing and that something was not right. Fortunately, the hours, days and the week ahead would become a drug-induced blur for me. I would live through it and I would suffer as each complication unfolded, but I would remember little. My mother, on the other hand, barely slept for the next seven days, the next 168 hours, yet she would remember it all vividly.

I moved from the PACU to the ICU around 10 p.m. An Intensive Care Unit at a Level I Trauma Center is unique and severe.

The patients around me were sedated, barely conscious, and in several cases, barely alive. There were no hospital gowns, only sheets to cover us patients, and there was an emergency operating room in the middle of the unit.

Seconds—not minutes, hours, days or years most of us take for granted—separated life from death in this ICU.

Fourteen tubes and attachments to my body were monitored on my own computer, watched carefully by a nurse who sat next to me the entire time. My parents came and went. They were allowed to visit me only 15 minutes each hour. Finally at 6 a.m., 24 hours following my initial move to pre-op, the doctors removed my dreaded breathing tube.

My post-surgery diet consisted of only ice chips. My throat was sore from the breathing tube and my mouth was dry to the point where it was not even sticky; my tongue felt like rubbing two dry fingers together. I was annoyed I was not allowed to have anything to drink. If I could eat ice chips, why could I not drink water? The juxtaposition irritated me.

Extra fluid from the surgery drained from my body through two chest tubes that had been inserted during surgery. My parents were told these tubes were normal for someone in my postsurgical state. Yet, these tubes would become my most painful and frustrating enemy. Used to drain excess blood and fluid, one tube entered my body through the space between my ribs, a space where a bundle of nerves also painfully resided. The open end of the chest tube lay between my chest wall and my lung to drain excess fluid that collected there. The other end of the tube was connected to a two-liter suction device situated right next to my body. Normally, a two-liter container is sufficient for the duration that the drainage tube is needed, usually two or three days. However, I drained two liters of fluid within the first 24 hours. The drainage container needed to be replaced.

Up until then, that was the most pain I had experienced in my life. But even that would be surpassed within the week.

Just before the tube entered my body it connected with a second tube. The nurse jiggled and yanked and struggled to separate the two, shaking the tube that went straight into my body. Not only did she wiggle a tube into an open wound that was bound on one side by a nerve-flanked rib, but also moved around a tube that stuck straight into a cavity in my side. It was horrible. I felt it and I could see the pain mirrored on my mother's face as she watched.

When I filled the replacement container again that evening, my drainage collection container, or Pleurevac, was changed in the same manner with an equal amount of pain. Maybe more. Because this time I knew it would hurt. I anticipated the pain and my body tensed to steel itself from the jiggling tube inside my body.

It became clear to my mom that disconnecting the drainage tubes was too painful for me. At my mom's request, the nurse increased the dosage of my pain medication. The Trauma I nurses were efficient and highly trained, but they did not appear to be comfortable dealing with parents who asked such frequent and detailed questions. During the 45 minutes my parents were not allowed with me, they spent their time on the phone with extended family members. These family members, who are also physicians, gave my parents a new list of questions to ask.

It was around this time when I started getting frustrated with being in San Diego. While Dr. Garfin was the best, the nurses were different from my nurses in South Bend. The South Bend nurses knew my name and my family, and they showed a unique level of care and concern. For the nurses in South Bend, the accident was their accident. Memorial Hospital of South Bend was a small town's hospital. The UCSD Medical Center was an institution.

At a huge facility in a city so near to the Mexican border, there were many nurses whose first language was not English. While I consider myself embracing of all cultures, we had to communicate with nurses who did not speak English well enough to communicate effectively with us. I needed someone who understood my needs and could communicate with them in Spanish. So we brought in the best bi-lingual physician we knew: Dr. Heather Vandeweghe.

Heather is a pediatrician at UCLA and works in public health clinics in inner-city Los Angeles. She is also my cousin.

My mom called Heather, and Heather said she would come down that night. She also told my mom and me to refuse to have the nurse change my drainage tube and insist that the doctor change it. This would anger the nurse she said, and it did, because it required the nurse to call the doctor down to the ICU.

Heather knew that in pediatric care the drainage tube was changed at the site where the tube enters the collection container instead of near the body. We did not know it could be done that way. Apparently neither did the nurses. Either that or they would not—could not—deviate from written orders. Thankfully, when the doctor arrived, he did that for them. "Yes, change it at the site of the container. Of course!"

The nurse was not pleased. But my life became much more comfortable. And I learned a valuable lesson from my cousin: You can say "No."

Two hours later, Heather walked in as though it was her own hospital, wearing her white coat embroidered with "Dr. Vandeweghe." She may have annoyed the hospital staff with attention to my concerns, but I know my parents were always more comfortable when she was there reading my chart, talking to the nurses or asking questions to the doctor on call. She became my advocate and, in a way, our interpreter. Medical rhetoric is its own language, and I have a feeling that it is often misunderstood in typical doctor-patient discussions.

At some point after surgery, Dr. Garfin came to tell me that he had not been able to straighten my spine. I do not remember this conversation, or maybe I did not want to remember it. While everyone around me knew that my surgery had not been a success, all I knew was that my body was draining fluid from a painful chest wound, and that we had neither the rapport nor communication with the medical staff in San Diego that we had experienced in South Bend. The prognosis for my back, and my future, was uncertain. But at that time, I was not thinking beyond the next 15 minutes when my parents could visit.

Something disconcerting was coming into focus: Rock bottom.

17

The next several days were filled with tubes, IVs and Jackie Collins. I continued to drain at least two liters each day. My drug and chemistry levels were tested repeatedly, and I was stuck so often my arms looked like someone colored them with a black Sharpie pen. Finally, when there was nowhere left to poke, a catheter called a "central line" was placed into the large jugular vein in my neck and stitched to the skin to create constant access for all my intravenous needs. What a nightmare that was! It was all function and no compassion. I cannot remember if it was a nurse or a doctor, or some sort of technician, who cut my neck to insert the catheter, but I bled and bled during the procedure, and no one bothered to clean it up. Blood ran down my neck and dried to a matted crisp in my hair. Still in the Rotobed, I would have been thrilled with South Bend's rinseless soap. But I did not even get a wet napkin. Thank goodness for my mother. She did her best to wipe away the blood and then, I am sure, gave someone bloody hell for it.

Our only entertainment during this time was Jackie Collins novels. Not normally my first choice of literature, this mindless "fluff," as we called it, got me through the toughest week of my life. What could be better for a college girl than Jackie Collins, especially the steamy love scenes? My mom read to me for hours: *Hollywood Wives*, *Hollywood Husbands*...we read every *Hollywood* book she wrote. Even when I drifted off to sleep and my mom stopped reading, I would wake up from the absence of hearing her lulling voice. Often times she had to backtrack by sentences and paragraphs, even pages, to the last part I remembered, while the nurses gathered outside my privacy curtain to listen. This was good stuff and the nurses liked it too.

At some point each day my father would come to relieve my mother. She would return to my uncle's condo to shower and change. One time she tried to sleep, but it was never long before my dad would call her and ask when she was returning. My father, my dad who loves me so much, could not handle seeing me so beaten. Women are stronger that way. Women are also better at reading Jackie Collins.

More than once that week, my father sat down and asked me if there was anything he could do.

"Read," I said, shifting my eyes toward the book. "Mom marked the page where we left off."

Dad picked up the book, looked at it and looked at me. It was not a genre he was comfortable reading, especially to his 18-year-old daughter. He watched *Beverly Hills, 90210* and *Melrose Place* with me the remainder of the summer, but watching television and reading the words in a book were different.

"This? You want me to read this?"

"Yes, Daddy," I said. "We are at a good part."

"Oh, Haley, are you sure?"

I nodded and he started reading as the nurses gathered outside the curtain again. He read quietly.

"Louder please, Daddy." I could not hear him over the dull roar of the Rotobed's motor.

For a college girl isolated in a hospital room, with no love interests and no social life, there was little chance for me to enjoy my college time as others might. But I could read about it.

Dad, however, could not. He would get to the good part, and suddenly, the two who were huddled with little clothing to share warmth in the narrative were headed to get something to eat. What? What happened? What was up with that?

"Daddy," I complained, "you skipped over it."

Sigh.

He relented, backtracked, and read the sex scene, very mechanically, very quietly and very quickly. I think this was Daddy's rock bottom too. This went on for five days.

Thank goodness for Jackie Collins…

On Monday, June 8, six days past the surgery that did not straighten my back and left me near road kill physically, I finally did hit rock bottom. The chest tubes were still in and the fluid still poured out of me. It was now more than an annoyance; it was a medical issue that needed to be addressed. Two liters a day, for six days, was not normal.

The doctors determined that a lymphatic duct—a small five millimeter vessel that runs the length of the spine through the chest and carries lymph, a fluid containing immune factors—had been cut during surgery and needed to be repaired. This created two issues: One, an additional surgical procedure was required; and two, from which point in the duct was the leak coming? The latter would determine the extent and seriousness of the former.

In order to visualize the vessel, which cannot be seen easily on simple X-ray or CAT scan, I needed a radiologic procedure called a lymphangiogram. I was wheeled into an X-ray room and laid onto a table, without my brace on. I still had the large kyphosis, or camel hump, on my swollen and sore back, and I had to lie on a cold, hard X-ray table. Had I not been scheduled for surgery and general anesthesia the following morning, I would have been fully anesthetized for this procedure. Instead, I received only some intravenous narcotics and topical drugs to dull the pain. A lymphangiogram was rarely performed this way, but there was hesitation to put me through general anesthesia on two consecutive days. I had a doctor and a nurse who stood next to me the entire time. Their sole purpose was to monitor my pain and vitals. When the morphine stopped working the doctor ordered, and the nurse administered, the change from morphine to Demerol.

Two additional doctors, one of them a resident (a doctor in training), cut the top of each of my feet in order to stitch in two tubes, one into my right and one into my left lymphatic system. Each doctor handled one foot. The attending physician made a small, precise incision requiring only two stitches. The resident was not as practiced, so the cut (and future scar) was noticeably larger. As my mom watched the blood flow from the holes in my feet, the irony of my suffering for a greater cause was not lost on her. "Please wipe the blood off her feet! Please wipe the blood off her feet!" She pleaded silently in her head, unable to speak for fear of upsetting me. She too hit rock bottom on this day and was paralyzed with her own exhaustion and emotional pain.

Blue dye, which would be detectable on the fluoroscopic X-rays, was injected through the tubes in my feet to travel throughout my body's lymphatic system. The location of the disruption in my lymphatic system would be manifest by evidence of a leakage of dye on the X-ray. I had to lie still while waiting for the dye to make its way through my body, and then I had to continue to lie still as a series of X-rays were taken to follow its progress.

Not since the night of the accident had I been that cold and in that much pain. Nausea came and went. Another click, another X-ray.

"Stay still," I was told.

I shivered.

"Do not move," the instruction came.

This continued for three hours, with my mother allowed next to me—to wipe my tears from my cheeks, but not the blood off my feet—only when they were not taking pictures.

The results of the test produced good and bad news. The good news was they found the problem, the site where the lymph duct was cut during surgery. Because this thoracic lymph duct ran parallel to the spine, cutting it had almost been inevitable. The bad news was that it needed to be repaired.

More surgery.

I knew it was coming, but I did not understand the extent. Initially this short two-hour operation was designed to reinsert new rods in my back. But the development of the damaged lymph duct required a surgical fix.

Another anterior approach.

Another surgery from the front.

Another nine-hour journey to the edge, with additional unknown dangers, one of which had already happened in the form of a leaking duct.

All I kept hearing was, "You don't want to go through it twice...."

But twice it was.

By the morning of June 9, the day of my last planned surgery, I was exhausted, black and blue, and fully aware that I had little strength left. I was terrified. The two surgeries in South Bend immediately after the accident were no-brainers; they were necessary in order for me to have the slimmest chance to walk. That gamble paid off. My third operation, the first one in San Diego, was relatively short and was required to prevent an infection where the rods had broken through my skin. Surgery number four was long and unsuccessful, even harmful, and I had been traumatized with fear as the anesthesia had worn off.

The fifth time I knew what was coming: a Mack truck headed straight for me. Again.

I was frightened when I went into the pre-op room. My cousin Heather promised she would be in Recovery when I woke up. That was comforting to me, and even more so for my parents. But I was no longer naïve and no longer brave. As I was wheeled away from my parents to the operating room, I tried my best not to cry. It did not work. Tears flowed as I cried out loud watching my parents appear farther and farther away. I was scared. The room where I was prepped for surgery was cold, and I was so frightened I started to shake. This was the last time. It had to be.

I called to anyone who would listen, to anyone within earshot, and begged them to have this be my last operation. I begged them to fix my lymph duct *and* complete the insertion of the new instrumentation:

"Please tell Dr. Garfin to do it all at once. Please tell him I can't do this again. Please, tell him to do it all this time." I pleaded over and over, "I can't do this again," until the gas mask was put on and I heard the music. Then I was out.

Once again, Dr. Winchell began the frontal approach, this time to fix the lymph duct. He deflated a lung, moved my stomach and cut off the flow of major blood vessels. He did this with few, or no, complications. The X-rays from the horrible day before pinpointed exactly where the duct leaked, and it was repaired quickly.

Then, it was Dr. Garfin's turn. His final turn.

And my last chance.

He had said he would never have risked this second frontal operation just to make another attempt to straighten my spine. It was too risky and the chance for success was even slimmer than the week before. Apparently, it is never easier the second time. But since Dr. Winchell was going in anyway, and the risk of the surgery was unavoidable—the lymph duct simply had to be fixed for me to survive—Dr. Garfin took advantage of this second chance.

My parents again waited for more than eight hours. My mom called Heather several times to confirm she was coming. My mom called Coach Tim Welsh to share her fear that I might not make it. Coach alerted everyone at Notre Dame and the prayers began. He and Missy Conboy made plans to come to San Diego. My parents sat right outside the operating room because the extra 20 feet to the surgery waiting room was too far for them.

Every time the doors opened they looked up, hoping only to hear that I was alive. It never occurred to them to hope for the miracle of a straightened spine. Even with the capable and hopeful Dr. Garfin it was a long shot, especially since it had failed the first time. My body was not healing right, and attempts to fix my spine had caused such damage and strain on the rest of me that my body was barely surviving. The goal of the surgery was just to fix the lymph duct and for me to be okay.

The hours passed. Dr. Garfin paused a final time after operating on me and Dr. Winchell stepped back up to the operating table to put things "back in place."

While Dr. Winchell was closing me up, Dr. Garfin came out to see my parents. Suddenly, there was no time to prepare—he moved toward them so quickly, with such authority—there was no time left to be nervous, no time to gauge his mood. It was obvious. Dr. Garfin's body language spoke volumes to my parents. My father hoped what he thought to himself to be true, "He looks like a kid on Christmas morning."

And he had the best present for which my parents could have hoped.

"Dr. Winchell is closing her up," Dr. Garfin said, beside himself with pure joy. "She's doing fine. He found the leak and it's tied off tight. I removed the donor bone and tried to reposition it."

The emotion was starting to show. He could not wait to get the words out. He sort of shook his head side to side, perhaps in marvel at what had just happened.

"Then, I shaved the bone graft like a pencil and when I reinserted it, her whole spine just popped straight!" Dr. Garfin proclaimed.

He paused to gather himself, to find the right words, and to put them in the right order. He wanted to speak a language my parents could understand.

"I am not sure what happened," Dr. Garfin continued. "Perhaps the week of the bone graft being in place stretched her back enough...she has very strong muscles. I don't know. But she'll walk tall. Her spine is straight."

My parents could not assimilate this news. Not just good news, but the best news. Dr. Garfin had gone where few surgeons had the skill or even bravado to go. He had pulled me back from the edge and left me, not just in better shape than he had found me, as he had done the first time, but at a point where I could, in time, walk back from that edge myself.

Finally good news, news to celebrate. We had all hit rock bottom and we knew life could only get better, but it was almost unfathomable to have it improve like this within hours.

Relief flooded my parents' hearts as tears filled their eyes. They had come so close to losing me twice; first the night of the accident when they had no control and no knowledge of what was happening until it was over. Then a second time, when they did have choices: which doctor, what medical facility, hours and hours of surgeries, trauma room care, intensive care, procedures and treatments.

They asked themselves so many questions. "Is it over? Finally? Can we see her to be sure? How do we say thank you to a man who has saved our child?"

18

Hope, relief, joy, exhaustion. My parents lived with emotions that either drained the life out of them or, like now, sent them to the moon and back with every breath. Lost in the euphoria was the harsh reality that while I might be on the right road to an eventual recovery, at the moment my body still had miles to go.

After Dr. Garfin briefly explained the developments to my parents, he went back into the operating room to finish what he had started. Two additional rods still needed to be inserted along the back of my spine to provide support. There were no complications. Surgery was over and all I had to do was heal. Rest, wait and heal. I do not remember much coming out of that last operation, except that my cousin Heather was there as promised. It was better already.

After the recovery room phase, I skipped the PACU and spent two days in the Intermediate Care Unit on the seventh floor. My mom's panicked phone calls to South Bend resulted in both Missy Conboy and Tim Welsh coming to visit. Missy came for a day and Tim stayed two. But they came, all the way from Indiana because we needed them, even though we did not know it. I was then moved back to where I started this adventure: to the 11th floor, called The Pavilion.

While my back was in the best shape it had been in since before the accident, my body was in its worst shape. And emotionally, I was barely hanging on. I still had my jugular venous line, but that did not prevent further needles from being stuck in my arms.

"We need to draw blood to check your oxygen level," a Dr. Gilbert told me, which could only be done from an artery. I found that highly annoying. The pain was still constant, but not in my back. It was the rest of my body that hurt, especially the hip from where the bone graft was taken. In addition to the cadaver bone used in my anterior fusion, my own bone was used for the posterior fusion. Dr. Garfin said he had given me a "matching scar" to mirror the previous hip bone removal done in South Bend.

One night, with Demerol still administered frequently through my PCA pump, the Notre Dame Leprechaun paid me a visit. Not the living school mascot who had visited me in South Bend, but the little guy: the trademarked side-profiled Leprechaun with his pointy shoes. He posed on the top of my curtain rods. I looked, blinked and looked again. Yes, he was there. It was interesting, but not frightening. There was a lady in the room, however, who frightened me. She stood in the corner, by the door, dressed in dark gray shabby clothes.

"Get her away! She's going to get me! Get her out!" I hissed at my mom, who was trying to sleep in the chair in my room.

"What? Get who?"

Afraid the unwanted visitor would hear me, I kept whispering sternly to my mom to get "that lady" away from me, to "make her leave!" And my mom, in her tired state, started to believe that there actually was someone in my room. But as she awoke fully, she realized that it had been about 40 minutes since my last dose of Demerol, and that the Leprechaun had appeared 40 minutes after the previous dose of Demerol. Okay, time for a new pain medication.

My second day on the 11th floor was equally eventful. My throat started to close and I felt like I could not breathe. It felt as though the central line in my neck was preventing the air from getting to my lungs. The pressure in my throat was building and building, until I was gasping for air.

"Mom! Mom! I can't breathe!"

My mom rang the red emergency button and rushed to the door to yell for help. The nurse came, took one look and called for a doctor from the phone in my room. He gave her a verbal order and she shot medication into my central line. Not into my arm, thank goodness.

My breathing had eased by the time Dr. Winchell and his interns arrived. They stayed to monitor me for 30 minutes. Then the nurse checked my output, as I was still catheterized after surgery. The diuretic had worked. "It's nothing," we were told.

Nevertheless, I was whisked away—downstairs or maybe to a different room on the same floor—for a series of tests to investigate the problem they described to us as "air in the chest." The central line was removed and I was declared "safe." Again, the doctors said it had turned out to be nothing.

"Nothing," was exactly what we wanted to hear. We did not need any additional complications; we did not need to think that anything else could go wrong. Nothing was the only explanation we could handle. But months later, while reading through medical records, my dad would learn what nothing was. Nothing had actually been my body in congestive heart failure. My heart had been so overworked by my body's fluid overload that it had gone into distress. As a family, we discussed this and tried to figure out if we had read my medical records correctly. We had.

Why, then, did no one tell us? Because they knew we could not handle it. If it could be corrected and controlled, then there was no need for us to know. We—not just I, but my parents too—had been through enough. It was a wise call on the part of my medical team. Surprising, but nonetheless the right decision for us. I had become more than a patient to them. I was a person, with a family, about whom they cared.

With my back straight, my new custom-fit brace and my "air-in-the-chest" problem fixed, I said goodbye to the Rotobed and stood up for the first time in more than two weeks. I was nervous that I would not be able to walk, that I would have to retrain my body again. But that was not the case. This was a different type of rehab. I could stand and I could walk, and even my bladder and bowel function returned quickly.

But it was a more painful and exhausting process this time. It hurt to walk, hurt to stand, hurt to sit. I just hurt with fatigue. I met once a day with a physical therapist, not twice daily as planned. And some days physical therapy had to be cancelled because I was just too tired. I had much more energy to push forward in the hospital in South Bend. As I neared the end of my time at the UCSD Medical Center, I barely had the energy to walk one lap around the nurses' station. But at least I walked straight.

Discharge day was awesome. I could not wait to get the heck out of there. Nancy and Angie had flown in to spend some time with me, and my dad was there to drive us back to the condo. Compared to San Diego, my time at Memorial Hospital had been a party. And that was how we would remember it: as a celebrated time, a time when I learned how to walk, a social event each afternoon with visitors and friends. By contrast, San Diego was lonely, isolated and painful in every way. I was anxious to retreat to the safety of my uncle's condo.

My Uncle Gary and Aunt Barbara Vandeweghe own a condo in Del Mar, just north of San Diego, which I moved back into on June 19, after the last surgery. It is about a half mile from the beach and we vacationed there every summer when I was a child. It was home away from home: familiar and comfortable for us until I was able to travel back to Phoenix. We had access to a pool and a short walking path. It was perfect for me. And the weather allowed me to spend time outside, which was healing in itself. Phoenix in the summer was much too hot. South Bend was much too humid for me, especially wearing my heavy brace. It was a blessing to have such a place to recover for the next six weeks. Del Mar was just right.

But while my surroundings were ideal and my insides were healing, my mental state deteriorated. I was as emotionally unstable as the earthquake, registering 7.4 on the Richter scale that hit the first weekend I was in the condo. It woke me up at 5 a.m., but more importantly it, and the several aftershocks that followed, reminded me that I was still unbalanced on my feet. Falling was not an option. I needed to stay still. In order to heal, Dr. Garfin required me to stay lying down 23½ hours a day. I could not again go through what I just had survived. I barely made it through the first time. God sent the earthquake to remind me to stay off my feet.

June 24 marked five months since the bus accident. Five months, five surgeries. That particular day, my sister came to visit and was getting ready to go to the beach with a friend. I cried. I cried almost every day, it was just a matter of why. That day it was the beach.

I loved the beach. I loved the sand, the warm sun, the cool breeze. I loved swimming in the ocean, boogie boarding, body surfing and the salty water. I used to love catching huge waves, crashing underwater and having the current throw me until the wave passed. I had always felt safe under the water, never threatened. But never again would I be able to so recklessly let my body be tossed around. I would miss the excitement of being thrown to the bottom of the ocean, the sand in my suit and the salt in my nose. So many activities would now require me to be careful. When Laura, my ICU nurse in South Bend, told me that my life had forever changed, she really meant it. I had just not wanted to accept it.

Mary Frances also wore my Notre Dame training suit that day. I had only worn it a few times before the accident, and it made me realize that I may never train that hard again. Prior to college, I had never felt like part of a team. I happened to like the individuality of the sport of swimming. I had rarely concerned myself with my fellow teammates' times or training schedule or socialized with them outside of practice and swim meets. Pierre, my coach at the Phoenix Swim Club, always talked about caring for one another, but it never clicked with me. I remembered clearly how our assistant coach, Bil Kopas, once said he would have done anything for his former teammates at the University of Michigan. I had never understood that until I went to Notre Dame and swam for the Fighting Irish.

I spent hours thinking about and writing to my teammates. The swimmers on my team were incredible. They were people I wanted to be like. They cared, were sincere, and were genuinely good people. I loved going to practice with them, loved spending time with them. They became, before—but especially after—the accident, the most important people in my life. We trained so hard it hurt, and I loved it. I loved everything about it. How did I get so lucky to be a part of this school and the swim team? And then why was it taken away? I may never again be able to train hard, race fast, or swim butterfly. I finally felt like I belonged as a member of a team, yet in 1.7 seconds I was unable to do the one thing that had become such a huge part of my life. I couldn't be finished yet; I still had more to do, more miles to swim. I knew I should have been thankful to be alive and healthy and walking. And I was. But it still did not take away the loss I felt knowing I might never be the swimmer I used to be.

Thank goodness I still had my friends. My friends, my family, my school, my faith. I must have done something right to have ended up at Notre Dame, a place where all that really matters in life is valued most. But still, I was hoping that I would be able to swim again.

This thought was foremost on my mind when Susan Taylor, the CBS journalist from Arizona, visited to report on my progress. The interview lasted about three and a half hours. They filmed footage of me lying down doing physical therapy, walking around outside, and resting on the couch. I thought the interview went well. Susan asked about how I felt, how I was doing, how all the letters I received made a difference, and what I was looking forward to most. Before I answered the last question I took a deep breath, because I knew I would have a hard time answering it.

"Competing again," I said, barely holding it together.

But then Susan, very kindly but making a point, followed up with, "Yes, that is so important to you, isn't it?"

There was no holding it together. I burst into sobs and could only nod my head yes. I put my hands to my face and cried.

"I know. It is hard to think about," she continued.

"Then why did you make me?" I wanted to say, but I was unable to talk.

I was so angry and so emotional. Angry at myself for allowing myself to cry on camera, and emotional about the thought of racing again. Susan Taylor was not an unkind person; she just knew there was more to the story than I was willing to share. Yet as she had been trained to do, she drew it out of me.

Later, she would talk to my parents and say, "The audience is going to want to see her cry." My dad agreed, and the piece moved forward. To this day, it is the most complete and accurate newscast detailing my story. Yet it is the one I find most difficult to watch.

But thoughts of competing again did consume me. I envisioned it every night as I would lie awake. Often nights I was unable to sleep during those weeks in my uncle's condo, so I had a lot of time to visualize, to pray and to talk aloud to Meghan and Colleen. I knew when I finished my first race, no matter what my time or place might be, that I would have achieved my goal; the one thing most people did not think was possible. As soon as I touched that wall, I would win.

I always cried when I thought about my first competition, not just on camera but when I was alone as well. I knew it would definitely be at Rolfs Aquatic Center, home to the Notre Dame swimming team. Even if our first five swim meets were away, I would wait to swim at home. I wanted everyone to come. And I knew Meghan and Colleen would be there in spirit; I needed them there. They had helped me through so much; I knew they would stay with me until I reached my goal because, more than for anyone else, I was doing it for them. Then, I thought, this whole ordeal would be over. It could only be over when I was competing again.

While my nights were restless, filled with bathroom trips, aching legs and an emotional exhaustion that prevented me from sleeping, my days were not much different. Except during the day the mail came, the phone rang and there was good TV. "Good TV" meant soap operas and game shows, with an occasional nightly drama like *Beverly Hills, 90210* or *Melrose Place*. Both shows hooked my father, which warmed my heart and made me smile. On one ever-exciting night I actually guessed a "book and author" puzzle on *Wheel of Fortune* without any letter clues revealed, "*Swiss Family Robinson* by Robert Louis Stevenson." I was bored.

The phone calls came daily but there were only a few friends with whom I enjoyed speaking. These were the girls who did not talk to me with sadness or pity. They called and entertained me with funny stories, filling me in on silly gossip, like good friends do. There were the occasional questions about how I was feeling, but mostly our conversations were fun and lighthearted. It wasn't that they did not care because I knew they did. They called every day. For the most part, I knew they were hurting too, just as they knew I was. It was easy to talk about superficial and comical events, because each of us knew there was still pain inside.

When Jackie and Tim Welsh came to visit, Jackie told my mom the same thing. Jackie shared that it was nice to be able to laugh with my mom, because each of them knew there was still pain inside. It was not over, not for anyone. But we all found strength, solace and humor in each other's company. I was in a much better place physically than when Tim had visited me at the UCSD Medical Center. But this visit I was more depressed. I am not sure we ever used that word at the time, but it was clear I was depressed and tired.

For the three days Tim and Jackie stayed with us, I spent most of the time in my room. It was too hard for me to be around people. Not them, just people in general. I tried, but I was too worn down and still too emotionally unstable.

I much preferred receiving letters I could read and reread when I wanted. I could listen to the lives of others and be upset or envious that their lives had moved on, but no one had to know how I felt. I could read and retreat to my room to cry. I could look at the pictures they sent and cry some more. Sometimes I would read letters or look at pictures that I knew would make me cry, just because I felt like crying.

Despite my constant stream of mail, phone calls and visitors, I spent the summer feeling very lonely. I never liked talking about how badly I hurt, both physically and mentally, with my family or any of my friends, because I never wanted to burden them or have them feel sorry for me. I refused to accept pity or sympathy. I kept so much to myself and lived in a very Haley-centric world, thinking only of myself and how others affected my life.

There were times when I was overwhelmed by the generosity of others, but it was not until much later that I was able to fully appreciate the unconditional support I received. It was not until I was able to see beyond myself that I recognized there was a better way to live my life, a more caring way, a more selfless way. Through the selflessness of others I learned who I wanted to be, but I was not there yet.

My personal growth and spiritual journey were ongoing, though not as noticeable to me at the time. Only in reflection was I able to see how my life had changed. All the time I waited for my life to return to "normal," it never occurred to me that normal would never happen. Normal was in my life's rearview mirror, and I longed for what normal had been. But I had passed that place and reached a point of no return. All I could do was keep moving forward at a sustainable pace, and try not to live in a past that wasn't so great anyway. I had to create a new normal. I had the opportunity to create a new self, a new life: one that embraced my sorrow instead of pushing it aside. It would take years, but the roots began to grow that summer.

Yet I was still careful with whom I explored this new self. When I felt like talking about God, I turned to those who I knew would be accepting of my growing faith: Father Blantz, a history professor at Notre Dame; Sister Kathleen, the rector of my dorm; and the nuns at Xavier, my high school in Phoenix. Only with them did I feel comfortable sharing my deepest and youngest thoughts of God's plan for my life. I knew God was with me; I had felt His presence since the night of the accident. He had sent me to some really low places, but I took such comfort in knowing that God would always take care of me, that He was on my side. God is on the side of all of us, but I was blessed to have really felt it. My strength from day to day came from Meghan and Colleen, but I was learning it was God who worked through them.

By July 24, the six-month anniversary, I was healing nicely. The bruises and scabs on my arms from the multiple IV lines had healed, as had the holes in my torso where the chest tubes had been. For a month my mom had stuffed these holes with cotton, so they would heal from the inside out. Because they were an open cavity to inside my body, they could not heal topically.

Best of all, when I met with Dr. Garfin that day, he reported that there was no movement with my bone graft, that all tests and X-rays indicated my spine was fusing solid. I still had to be patient and careful, but I was much further along in the healing process than I had been six weeks post-op in South Bend, when my bones had already shifted and my spine had started to collapse.

I was also allowed to start sitting for as long as my back could tolerate, including a 10-15 minute car ride each day. We immediately went to Golden Spoon, my favorite frozen yogurt store. But that was enough. I was exhausted.

There was one downside to my appointment with Dr. Garfin. He did not want me to return to Notre Dame for the fall semester. I knew that was a possibility. Dr. Garfin had always been open and honest about my delicate back, and how devastating another failed fusion would be. He wanted me to stay at home through the end of the year to give my back its best chance to heal. I agreed. I too wanted to give my back its best chance to heal, but I knew that would happen at Notre Dame. On that point, we differed. But our mutual admiration for one another allowed us to part that day with an agreement to discuss it at my next appointment. I think he just wanted to delay disappointing me, but I remained hopeful.

I was also scared. What if I could not return to school? I did not deserve that. I had not deserved any of it, but I had accepted it. I had dealt with it and I had tried not to complain too much. But I also needed to go back to Notre Dame. Many of the reasons I had recovered so well were in South Bend. No one else understood what it was like being in an accident like we were. As soon as we crashed, an immediate force bonded us together: the women swimmers with one another, with our coaches, with the guys' team and with the entire school. That bond was intense and powerful; it helped me overcome so much. It enabled me to walk again and to gain the strength I needed to return to school after Spring Break. I did not do that by myself, the love of the people at Notre Dame did, Meghan and Colleen did, and they would do it again. They wanted to do it again, but I needed to be at Notre Dame for that to happen. I needed to be with everyone who shared that bond with me. I just needed to convince Dr. Garfin of that.

My cousin Heather and her husband, Kevin, came down from Los Angeles one weekend to visit. As with all visitors, my mom made them watch every VCR tape of video coverage and newscasts from the accident and my surgeries. Maybe they wanted to; I know my mom did. It annoyed me that my mom used any excuse to turn them on. Yet I had a strange fascination as well. I could not keep myself from watching each picture of Colleen and Meghan, each picture of the bus, each newscast. Except for the one where I cried. During that one, I always left the room.

Seeing the pictures of Meghan and Colleen on the television often led me to think about death. This usually happened late at night when my legs ached, when I had taken the maximum dose of pain medication and when my thoughts were a random and profound stream-of-consciousness: We all die. To so many death is sad, but it happens to everyone. I am going to die. How? Will people grieve for me? When will the people I love die? Death for Meghan and Colleen was so sudden and unpredictable and tragic, and hopefully painless. Will it be the same for me? Death is so hard to understand. And life is so short. When you really think about it, life and death are so hard to understand. Why? What does it all mean? Why are we here? I guess to be happy and to make others happy. Maybe Meghan and Colleen died because they had already made so many people happy. But their death made all those people sad. I just don't get it. No matter how awful it is, and how sad it makes people, it still happens and it always will. People often say, "no one can live forever," but do they really think about what that means? I usually fell asleep sometime after I had exhausted myself with thoughts of death and realized that it was all too deep for me.

My last two weeks in San Diego were filled with more of the same: sleepless nights with random thoughts and letter writing, and endless days with stacks of mail, short outings and television. Thank goodness for the Summer Olympic Games in Barcelona, Spain. It gave me something good to watch.

19

I had a lot to look forward to as I traveled to the 115-degree heat in Phoenix on August 3. Sitting in the San Diego airport with both my parents, I looked around and thought about how normal everyone else's life was, or how normal their lives appeared at a glance. Families returning home after a beach vacation, children with SeaWorld "Shamu" stuffed animals, business travelers with rolled up shirtsleeves and briefcases. Did any of them have any idea what I had just been through? Three weeks of surgeries and six weeks of lying down recovering. Not your typical summer in San Diego. But then again, nothing about my life was typical. Would it ever be? I often asked myself that question.

What would life be like if this had not happened? Where would I be and what would I be doing? In what ways had this changed my life? I usually had to stop myself from thinking about it because there was never a concrete answer. All I knew for sure was that if this had not happened, I would be getting ready to head back to Notre Dame for my sophomore year. But of course, I was not. Reality was painful.

I was uncomfortable sitting in the airport, but I did not want to tell my parents. I knew they were concerned that the hour-long flight would be exhausting for me. And they were right, it would be. It already was. Just the 25-minute drive to the airport was more activity than I had done in months. But I could not wait to get home to my own bed, my own room and my own phone line. Hopefully a little bit of my own life back. Friends could visit. My mom could visit friends. I knew she wouldn't, but it would be nice to have a break from her. She needed a break from me too, I was sure. I needed my space. I always had. Especially then, after seven months of needing her for everything, I was ready for a little independence.

When I was growing up my mom used to joke that she would go to college with me and rent an apartment near campus. Then look what happened. She always said, "Be careful what you ask for."

She should have listened to her own mantra. Not that this was her fault. But at times, when I was depressed and lashed out at her in anger, it helped to have someone who would love me no matter what I said to her, no matter how ridiculous my rant.

When we got off the plane in Arizona a camera crew was waiting. It was 1992, and pre-9/11, so they met us at the gate. I turned on my happy face like you would turn on a television. I was happy on the outside, but inside I was in a lot of pain. It was times like these when my mother would remind me that no one wanted to hear about the pain. They wanted to hear how well I felt and how well I was doing. So I responded to questions with answers like, "It is great to be home," and "I am so grateful for everyone's support," and "I feel pretty good." The first two were true, but the third was the continued emergence of my dual persona.

Home was home, but I was exhausted and slept most of the afternoon. When I woke up, I counted the minutes until Lorrei's arrival the following day: August 4, my 19th birthday. 19-years-old. My life had changed so much in one year. It was a mixed-emotions milestone. My last year as a teenager, yet I was so far from that. I celebrated all I had achieved in one year, and mourned all I had lost.

I had not seen Lorrei all summer and she looked good. Her tanned, healthy and well-rested body contrasted with mine, which was pale, tired and held together with rods and a back brace. What different summers we had experienced. My mom knew how important Lorrei's visit was to me, so she tried her best to make my teammate feel welcome. Very rarely did my mom focus her energy or attention on someone besides me. But when it was someone who could help me, she found it in herself to do so. And I was grateful. Grateful to have my friend feel so welcomed in my house, and grateful to have my mother's attention diverted elsewhere. She even baked Lorrei her own cake for my birthday, chocolate with chocolate frosting, which contrasted with my white cake with raspberry filling.

Spending the week with Lorrei was good, but I was more tired than I wanted to be. I wanted to have fun with her. Or more importantly, I wanted her to have fun with me. We did little beyond sitting, talking and lying out in the sun. I was so scared my friends and teammates would return to school later that month and forget about me. Silly fears, but very real for me with all that had transpired. I had visions of the team training together, eating dinner together, hanging out and having fun together—all without me. And when that would happen, it was tough to hear about. When classes resumed and I was still in Arizona, I couldn't help but call every day to keep in touch. But what I did not know until later was that they longed for me to be there just as much.

I kept busy at home, trying not to worry too much about my upcoming set of X-rays. Dr. Garfin, after much pleading and begging on my part, agreed to consider allowing me to return to school if my next X-rays showed signs of fusion.

"We wouldn't want your back to not heal again," he had said, and he knew I agreed. But I just really needed to get back to Notre Dame.

Gerry Seaquist, my high school swim coach, asked me to help him coach when Xavier's practices began in mid-August. It was hot and I was never able to stay longer than an hour, but I enjoyed being back on the pool deck, interacting with swimmers, some of whom I had swum with as a student. It was nice to have something to do each day. Even one outing was exhausting, especially an outing that kept me outside. Arizona in August was hot and humid. But I was determined and stubborn, and I needed the mental stimulation more than my body needed another hour of rest.

That August while coaching at Xavier, I got my first glimpse of God's plan. I did not know it at the time, but I can see now—and feel lucky to have this insight—that my suffering from the bus accident was not in vain. There was a sophomore swimmer at Xavier that fall, Wendi, who had been in a car accident over the summer. I met her the first day of practice and we connected instantly. Her parents asked me to talk with her about what it was like to lose a close friend because Wendi's best friend was killed in her car accident. It was hard for me. I still had difficulty talking about Meghan and Colleen and I was not sure what to say. How could I console her when I was still dealing with my own emotions? The best I could do was to say, "I understand," and "I know what you are going through and it's hard." There are not many people who can say that truthfully, so perhaps just my honest, sympathetic words were enough to comfort.

I also listened. I had done so much talking about my own accident that it was my turn to listen. It was strange, for the first time, to hear someone say "the accident" and know she was not talking about my bus accident. As odd as it may sound, it was eye-opening for me to discover that other accidents happen. The details may be different, but the lives are equally changed. The grief Wendi felt for the loss of her friend was no less than my grief for Meghan and Colleen. I understood all her emotions.

I was also given the opportunity to understand someone else's physical challenges. Coach Tim called to tell me about an incoming freshman swimmer, Ry Beville, who also had been in an accident over the summer. His injuries were much different than mine; he had bleeding on the brain. But the effects were similar: he had limited movement on the right side of his body and was told he would recover in the hospital for up to a year. Coach Tim asked me to call him. Of course I would. I had received hundreds of phone calls when I was in the hospital and each one of them meant so much. This was my chance to repay the favor, and it was my honor to do so. Every couple of days, I called Ry's hospital room and told him to prove the doctors wrong. I had, and I told him I knew he would too. And he did. He was at Notre Dame and swimming by the spring semester. I do not know if my words actually helped him, but at least I felt as though I had tried to help. And I was glad to have something to take my mind off the upcoming set of X-rays.

Nancy and I spent most of August together. She had been in San Diego with me for a month and she was, at times, the best and only medicine to ease me through this difficult and boring time. We watched television together, she painted my toenails when I could not reach them and often we just hung out doing nothing. But when she left Phoenix to return to St. Mary's College in South Bend, I knew summer was over. Her departure left a hole in my days and was a painful reminder that everyone else—my teammates, my roommate and my friends—were returning to school as well.

They would all be together soon, but without me. I felt like I was being punished, like I was not allowed to see my friends. Of course I was thrilled that my back was healing, but it continued to be a difficult time for me emotionally. Phoenix would always be my home, but I belonged at Notre Dame. All my friends were there. My life was there. But I was not. I hated the accident for keeping me away from the one place where I was truly happy. I kept telling myself, and I truly believed that the most important thing was for my back to heal. But that did not mean I had to be happy about being away from my friends. They were all together and I was alone. I cried at night when I thought about it. The team was my strength and I needed them. A part of me was missing. My stomach felt hollow.

It was a lesson in reality that sometimes I cannot have everything even if I really want it. And, as I told myself daily, as much as I wanted to go back to school, my back came first. I tried to believe that. I really wanted to. I felt as though I must have done something right in my life for God to have blessed me with His love in so many ways, seen and unseen. But I clearly still had some lessons to learn.

On the 24th of August I again took note of the date. Would a 24th ever go by without me thinking about the accident? I used to count weeks, late each Thursday night. Then it was months. And there would come a time, I was sure, when I would honor the accident only by the year. But it was hard to imagine that time would come. I hoped that eventually the accident would not control my life to the point where I was counting days and months. I spent most of the day on August 24 talking to my mom about the night of the accident, reliving what happened during the following days and talking about all the miracles (big and small) that had happened since.

There were nights, most nights, when my emotions took over my physical self. Dr. Garfin had prescribed a sleeping pill, but it rarely worked and seemed to only make me more delirious and out of control. At night, my legs were such a dichotomy of pride and anger. I tried to keep in perspective how proud of them I was, how thrilled I was that I could walk and use my legs again. But most nights they bothered me. They would ache and tingle and make it impossible for me to fall asleep. The nerve damage literally drove me crazy. It was unbelievably frustrating to be unable to fall asleep when I was so tired. And while my restless legs were not painful, I found

back pain easier to manage. Sometimes, when I was beyond exhausted and slightly out of my mind, I would bang my legs against the
wall next to my bed. The sting of the wall on my legs dulled the tingling and the aches. The pain of slapping my own legs was something I could control, and it was the one thing I could do that would
focus my attention away from the tingling and toward my self-
inflicted pain.

During these nights my mother would stand outside my room
and cry, knowing what I was doing to myself. She felt out of control
too and knew there was nothing she could do, yet again, to ease her
daughter's pain. She knew I needed to be by myself so she never
came into my room, but she couldn't leave the hallway either. She
was torn. Her heart was breaking again.

I was in my own world of pain, and in my own way I had to figure out how to get out. I hated the uncertainty, yet that was all my
life was: uncertain. Nothing was solid (though hopefully my back
was getting there) and my mind was far from stable. The lack of
sleep did not help and at times the only thing I could do was cry.

While my nights were spent in a restless, leg-banging, sleeping-
pill-induced sleep, my days were tired and depressed. Most of the
time I was not happy. Friends and acquaintances who stopped by
tried to make me feel better and complimented me on everything I
had been through, but that only made me cry. I do not know why.
Maybe I was too tired to politely thank them or maybe I was too
tired to relive the story of my living hell. Or maybe I was crying tears
of joy. Joy that I was alive, joy that I was walking and joy that one
day I would be healed. I guess I was just so emotional that anything
made me cry, and I was too tired to suppress my emotions.

I began seeing a psychologist, Dr. Herbert Collier, during the
time I was at home. At the time, I did not feel like I needed this therapy. How much more could I talk about the accident? But I felt like
I should. Dr. Collier said I had many emotions bottled up inside, feelings that I did not acknowledge, express or deal with. He was probably right, but I did not know how to express what I was feeling. The
pain, fear, sorrow, loss, anger and frustration were all too hard to talk
about. Ultimately it added up to depression. I was just not happy. I
wanted to be a normal college student. I wanted my old life back. I

wanted Meghan and Colleen back. But it was not going to happen. None of it.

At school, while the swim team practiced and started classes, they also thought about me. Daily phone calls from my teammates and classmates, now sophomores, with details of their lives were helpful and hurtful at the same time. Listening to Lorrei and Angie, or Cara and Amy talk about the swim parties and team dinners was hard, but I was desperate to know, desperate to stay in touch and desperate to be there. Cara and I had two classes together that semester and she told our professors that I would be returning shortly. They either wanted to believe my optimism expressed through Cara or simply could not make sense of my situation either. Everyone was hurting, and we all had feelings we had to sort through in our own way.

Assistant Athletic Director Missy Conboy, and Sister Kathleen Gilbert, my academic-athletic advisor, arranged to have my fall semester textbooks and syllabi sent to me in Phoenix. When the box arrived, I was overwhelmed by the number of books and the amount of work I would have to do to keep up. I was exhausted. How could I read and focus on so much academic work? My only consolation in this was realizing that maybe I was better off at home. Maybe Dr. Garfin was right; school was too much. I knew all I could do was try and that was what I resolved to do. The accident and my injury had been such a setback and such a lesson in giving up control. But this I could control. I had to challenge my mind academically. My body had been physically tested and I had overcome those trials. I would overcome this one as well. I started slowly and did the best I could to read and focus.

After weeks of anticipation, my X-rays were taken and sent to California. Then it was a waiting game. Two days, three days. It seemed like three months. I could not get them out of my mind. I could not get the accident out of my mind, although at times it was one thought removed.

Whenever I would think about something, a book or a television show or a restaurant, my thoughts always related back to the accident. Anything I did, I knew I was doing because of the accident. I had no control over the power of the accident. I hated not having control of my life and control of what was going on inside me. I could rest and eat as much calcium as I could tolerate, but that still would not guarantee that my bones would heal. Thank goodness I had such a stable family. My life and body were so indecisive that I was thankful I did not have to worry about anything else. Even though I did.

When the call came, Dr. Garfin announced that he and several other doctors agreed there were signs of fusion. He sounded thrilled and the tone of his voice told me I was well on my way to healing. This time correctly, straightly, and for good. As soon as I got off the phone, I immediately prayed in thanksgiving. Even with all my physical exhaustion I was healing on schedule, even ahead of schedule. All my patience and boredom had paid off.

But still no school. Not yet. Dr. Garfin wanted to see me one more time before he allowed me to return. He had his own schedule and I had mine.

"No pressure," I told Dr. Garfin, "but I have to go back sooner rather than later."

I know he wanted me to be at Notre Dame as much as I did. But more than anything, I knew we both wanted my back to heal. And it was finally doing so.

I called Coach Tim, who had been trying to call me as well. When we finally connected, he had plan-changing news. I had won the Spirit of Notre Dame Award. Sponsored by Maxwell House and General Foods, the award was given annually to one undergraduate and one graduate student. The respective company presidents would be at Notre Dame to present the award to a graduate student and me during the halftime of the Michigan vs. Notre Dame football game the following weekend. I had to be there, which meant I had to go see Dr. Garfin.

The night before my mom and I flew to San Diego, Meghan and Colleen sent me a sign. As I was lying in bed, something kept blowing in my room. I kept hearing a paper rustle. Then the piece of paper flew onto my bed. I turned on the light and saw it was the team roster. I knew then it was a sign that I would be with them soon. With that, I was able to fall asleep.

Sitting in Dr. Garfin's office the next day, I was so nervous I broke into a cold sweat. Also in the waiting room was an elderly lady who told my mom and me about the back surgery she was about to have. It was similar to what I had, and Dr. Garfin was doing it.

"You are in great hands," I told her.

Then she pulled out an article about me from the *San Diego Union-Tribune*, which she had laminated, and asked, "This isn't you, is it?" I smiled and said yes. I could see her physically relax having met me and seeing how well I was doing. I was glad I could comfort her, for I myself was paranoid, excited and, ultimately, scared.

For once, my mom offered little comfort. She had her own emotions with which to deal. While she was happy for me, she told me that whatever the outcome of today's meeting with Dr. Garfin, it would be her loss. Either I was going back to school and leaving her, or I was staying at home and not healing as quickly as we had hoped. I looked at her for a moment, not knowing how to respond. Silence was best. Sometimes I did not understand her.

But I understood Dr. Garfin clearly. He said I looked great. Healthy, happy, tan and upbeat. He did some neurological testing, which included checking my reflexes and pin-pointing for numbness, and said, "Your spinal cord is happy."

I smiled.

He looked at my X-rays and said my back was healing "exceptionally well" for being only three months post-surgery.

Then he asked me, "Well, what do you want to know?" He knew.

The words jumped out of my mouth as though they needed oxygen to survive.

"Can I go back to school?"

But before he had a chance to answer, my mom chimed in, "Don't let her go unless you are absolutely sure."

Thanks Mom.

Dr. Garfin explained to us that his main concern was not my going to class or overdoing it; he was only concerned with what might happen to me because of circumstance, because of being away from my cocoon of a life.

"If you were at home with Mom and Dad, I would have no hesitation about letting you go back to class," Dr. Garfin said.

Ugh, I sighed. I can't go.

"But being at school," he continued, "you probably won't do anything differently than if you were at home, so…"

So. So? So what?

"So," he said in a professional, confident tone, "you may go."

I was so excited. And relieved.

20

We flew back to Notre Dame on a Friday night. Angie and Lorrei picked my mom and me up at the airport, and we met Tim and Jackie Welsh for a quick dinner. I was tired and knew I had a big day on Saturday, so after dinner we went straight to Lyons Hall.

Sister Kathleen Beatty hugged me, and my mom was immediately relieved to remember how comforting Sister K was to us both. Mom knew Sister K would take care of me once she returned to Arizona. My room was again on the first floor, right across the hallway from Lorrei, Julie Schick, Angie and her roommate, Beth. Again, it was set up when I arrived. It was so good to be home.

I did not sleep well that night. I was either too excited or in too much pain, or maybe both. By early Saturday morning, I had taken a sleeping pill and six little green pills to help me sleep and to numb my tingling legs. But they did not help. My legs were horribly restless that night. Again, I vacillated between being angry and being grateful I could feel them at all. It was really annoying.

While awake, I thought a lot about the award I won, the Maxwell House Spirit of Notre Dame Award. What an honor! At a school where spirit and dedication are so apparent throughout the entire student body, it was an accomplishment to be singled out and recognized. What I wanted people to understand though, was that the award did not belong only to me, but to Meghan, Colleen and the entire swim team for what we had overcome because of our strength as a unit, not because of any of us individually. The spirit of Notre Dame was apparent in the lives of Meghan and Colleen, and it continued to live on through all of us.

I was uncertain I wanted to accept the award by myself, but I could not stop thinking about what Mr. Seaquist, Xavier's swim coach, had said. "Haley, so many of those people who will be in the stadium have been praying for you and inspired by you, and they would really love to see you accept the award. It would do them a lot of good to know that miracles happen with faith." Okay. That I could do. I would accept the award as a very public "Thank you."

I could not wait to see the team. After breakfast, Mom, Lorrei, Angie and I walked across campus to the swim team tailgater. It was a long walk and I was tired, but I was determined. My mom kept asking me to slow down or take a rest, but no amount of fatigue was going to keep me from seeing my teammates. Finally, when I got there, it was like I had never been gone. I felt right at home with old friends, even though I had only known these friends for one year. Their lives had moved on and continued while I was at home, but they had taken me with them.

The game was exciting. We tied Michigan 17-17 (before the days of overtime in college football) but I did not like sitting with my mother in the handicap section. Dr. Garfin worried about someone bumping into me or knocking me over, so I was not allowed to sit in the student section at football games. But being down on the field during the halftime presentation was exciting. Mom and Jackie Welsh watched from the sidelines; Cara Garvey, Kristin Heath and a couple of other swimmers came down to the bottom of the stands to wave hello and get a closer look. I just smiled, shook a lot of hands, and was in awe of the 50,000 fans cheering for me. It was inspiring. Of all people, I was chosen. It did not make up for all I had been through, but it was recognition of it.

Looking at pictures from the mid-field ceremony, I looked dazed, almost drugged. Whether it was all the medication I had taken at 5 a.m., the long flight from Phoenix the day before or the long walk across campus that morning, this was probably exactly what Dr. Garfin had worried about. Cara took a picture of Dick Rosenthal and me on the field at halftime. Dick had his hand on my arm and it looked like he was holding me up, or steadying me, or both. The picture hung in Dick Rosenthal's office until the day he retired as athletic director. I still have it hanging in my house, along with my field pass. The photo itself represents everything: my pain and fatigue, and Notre Dame's support.

I took only three classes that semester, as I had promised Dr. Garfin: Father Blantz's U.S. History class, Chemistry with Lorrei and Cara, and my sophomore Arts and Letters requirement: CORE. Cara was in that class with me as well. Thankfully, again, I did not have to make up most of the work I missed that first month. My focus was to keep up with current assignments and rest, which was easy to do because I had a lot of free time and was always tired.

My first week back on campus I did several interviews: the CBS affiliate in South Bend, ESPN radio, and the *New York Times*. Notre Dame's school newspaper, *The Observer*, ran an editorial about how I had finally returned to campus and how I exemplified the Notre Dame family. The publicity was draining, and it did not help my desire to forget about the accident and be a normal college student. But how else could I thank everyone who helped me? How could I not care about my support network when they had cared so much about me? And still did.

Eight months after the accident I was so moved to know how much people still cared. I would never forget that. Never again would I see a tragedy on the news and not deeply grieve for the months, even years, that lives would be changed because of it.

At Notre Dame it was no longer "my" accident. It was "ours." And "ours" meant there were a lot of different emotions and that we were all healing differently. I tried not to be frustrated with how others dealt with it, but it was hard. It was hard to see a teammate quit the team because she "just didn't want to swim anymore," when I would have given anything to swim. That was her choice, of course, and her way of healing. But it was something I did not understand, and it added to my frustration.

Unknown to many of us, Scully, one of our captains that year, and Coach Tim decided that the team needed to discuss the accident, as a group, one last time. The newest class, the freshmen, was invited to share a glimpse into the world in which we existed. For they, too, were part of our team.

Tim talked first about our lives being like a book, and for each of us, the accident told a different story. We were each on a different page or in a different chapter of healing, and each was correct.

Everyone on the team was given an opportunity to share; some people did not, while some people shared more than necessary. All was allowed, all was acceptable, all needed to be said. That meeting accomplished two significant events: it helped the freshmen learn more about their teammates and to learn to care for us, and it allowed the rest of us to know that it was okay that we had not moved on. The accident was still a very real part of our lives.

I spent most of the fall semester resting, playing Nintendo, taking three classes and continuing to deal with the accident the best I could. I also spent a lot of time talking to Lorrei and Angie. We often times talked about the accident, although it seemed like few others did. But it was nice to know my friends understood that for me, this was not over. Lorrei and Angie also understood and shared many of my feelings of loss.

These talks confirmed why I needed to come back to Notre Dame: to be with my friends, my teammates who felt the same way I did and with whom I felt comfortable sharing my most personal and emotional thoughts. I am not an emotional person, but when it came to the accident, I could not help it.

Laughter was healing as well. And it was easier to laugh with friends who also shared my grief. We all enjoyed telling stories about Meghan and Colleen, laughing with them and not at them. Meghan, especially, had always been the first person to laugh at herself; she knew when not to take life too seriously. Both girls continued to teach us lessons in death, as in life.

I too learned to lighten up. Most of the year had been so serious for me; I was due for a break. I visited Lorrei over Fall Break and spent a week at her house, amid cornfields. Cornfields! I had never seen one and I found them beautiful, which Lorrei found hilarious. There was mutual healing in laughing together. There was also healing in seeing the world from a different perspective. God's beauty was all around me; I just needed to look.

The hardest event for me that fall came just before finals. The first week in December, the swim team left for the National Catholics Championship meet. No matter how much I had prepared for that day, it still hurt. I went to the pool with Lorrei and Angie for our team Mass, but left halfway through. I could not hold it in any longer and I had to cry. I wanted to go to National Catholics so badly! I felt so isolated, so alone. I should have been going too, but instead I stayed back to deal with my disappointment alone. I felt horribly guilty leaving Mass. Although no one would accuse me of abandoning the team, I should have stayed to support them as they never wavered in their support of me.

Clearly God was not done with me. There was still pain from which I had to learn. But learn what? I struggled with finding the meaning in my suffering. But that was a step, an improvement; because at least I knew my suffering was not in vain.

I channeled my emotions through writing. I continued to write in my journal and in a more public domain: Notre Dame's school newspaper, *The Observer*. I covered the men's and women's swimming teams that year. To borrow a quote from the movie *Grease*, "if you can't be an athlete, be an athletic supporter." I supported the team by providing extensive coverage of all swim meets, which had been sparse in prior seasons. Since I could not swim, at least I could be part of the team by tagging along for a byline. With my spiral notebook in hand, I wrote two articles a week: one before a swim meet and one after the meet. I was glad to give the teams some print space that did not involve a bus.

This is when I first met George Dohrmann, a sports editor at *The Observer*. George and I became friends and, at times, more than friends. He was easy to be with, funny, and someone around whom I could let down my guard. That did not happen very often. George treated me with respect and kindness, but did not necessarily cater to me the way others did. I liked that. I liked that he was concerned but did not baby me. He allowed me to be myself, and to not be okay all the time. Often times with others—my family, teammates and friends—it was as though I might break again. I was to be handled with kid gloves. But that only forced me to internalize my fear, my pain and my discomfort, so as not to worry them. George was not like that, and he would not let me be either. As I have learned in my life, he was there for me to learn from.

During one conversation, George and I started talking about the bus accident. I was slowly letting him into my sheltered world of emotions, but he retreated.

"Stop that," he said.

"Stop what?" I was confused.

"Stop talking to me like you are, 'Haley Scott, Notre Dame Swimmer.' I like the real Haley better."

I must have looked confused, because he continued.

"Your voice changes when you talk about yourself. It is like you are talking about a different person. I have seen you do it with others in interviews, but don't do it with me. Talk to me like you are just Haley."

I have never forgotten that. Until that time, I had not realized that I went into "Haley Mode" when I spoke about the accident or my injury and recovery. I think it was a defense mechanism, a way to talk about something painful. My emotions were still so raw and I never liked to show much emotion to others. So to protect myself, I put up a wall and gave the facts, the platitudes and the truth the public wanted to hear. But very rarely did I show emotion. When I was interviewed by reporters other than George, my answers were carefully worded, almost rehearsed, always truthful, but almost scripted in order to keep control. Sometimes I still find myself in Haley Mode. But at least now I am aware of it and I try to be human as well.

George would go on to win a Pulitzer Prize for his newspaper writing at age 27. We would lose touch by then, although I would always follow his journalism career. He was blessed with the insight to see beyond an image and to get to the real story.

Over Christmas vacation, the team trained at Arizona State University for 10 days. I was thrilled to host the team in my hometown and thrilled with the news I received from Dr. Garfin. I was allowed to start back in the water and begin to wean my body off the brace.

At first I was disappointed that I was not allowed to take off my brace and throw it away. But I did not understand, until I first stood up without my brace, how dependent I was on it. I had no back muscles. For a year the brace held my body upright; it had not worked on its own. I was given a "t-brace" as we called it, although I am sure there is a more medically correct name for it. It was a much smaller brace that looked like a metal "t" on my torso. Or a cross. It allowed my back muscles to slowly develop without overstressing them.

I would wear this new "t-brace" for three months, on and off, but not in the water. In the water I could walk unaided. At Arizona State, in a pool where I had won so many state championship events in high school, I returned to the pool for the first time with a straightened back. This was the beginning. I had 10 months until my ultimate goal: competition.

1993. A new year. The Queen of England declared 1992 to be "annus horribilis." I could not agree more.

That January, I unknowingly began a ritual that would last for several years, though the details of the events would fade. I took note of each event that month and reflected on those same events from the year before: returning to Notre Dame after the training trip, starting spring semester classes, the freshmen spaghetti dinner—that we did not have to make because we were sophomores—and of course the upcoming one-year anniversary.

It was a tough week leading up to January 24, 1993. Most of us, my teammates and I, were emotional, sometimes crabby, and many lost control of their emotions. None of us knew what to expect from the approaching day. That same week an article appeared in *Sports Illustrated* to honor the one-year anniversary. It was well written and well received by almost everyone on campus, as well as readers, even those who did not care for Notre Dame.

For most of us who were on the bus, however, the article was difficult and upsetting to read. The pictures were too real and too vivid; I described them at the time as "tragically depressing." It was a tangible reflection of what I felt, and it was painful. I remember several people on campus stopping me that week with comments such as, "That was a great article in SI!" And it was great that we were still thought of and still cared about one year later. But there was nothing "great" about what happened. We would have much preferred not to be in *Sports Illustrated* for that reason. It was a highly charged, emotional week and Coach Tim recognized that. Once again we needed to gather and heal as a team. Our strength had always been together.

At midnight on January 23, 1993, the men's and women's swim teams gathered at the Grotto to pray. Wearing our unifying blue and gold Notre Dame swimming parkas, we stood in the cold under the glowing light of the Golden Dome and held hands. Our team captains led us in saying a Rosary, a prayer that carried us through the time of the accident: 12:17 a.m. The quiet but powerful words were chanted for almost 20 minutes. Our thoughts were in the same place, and in different places, as we reflected on that night and the year since. One year. The 24th. January 24.

When it was over, there was silence. Silent tears and silent hugs. There was little to say, but a lot to embrace. The silent spirit of our team that night was powerful.

Individually, however, many of us still struggled. I did. There were times when I could not handle or deal with my teammates' highly-charged emotions; I was still selfish that way. Yet I was also not strong enough to be by myself or around someone who did not, in some way, understand. Kevin was the perfect answer. He was not as emotionally attached to the accident as I was, but as a swimmer he had witnessed what the women's team, and I, had gone through.

Kevin helped me heal. We met almost every night in the Oak Room, a meeting space above South Dining Hall. He would listen, make me laugh and at times calm me down. He let me be sad, but he let me be happy as well; happy at a time when most everyone else was grieving and facing emotions they had bottled up for months. But for a year, I had lived with the accident and faced my emotions every day. Part of me wanted to celebrate the first anniversary, and Kevin allowed me to do that without guilt. I was happy to be alive, happy to walk and happy to be close to swimming again. My life had begun to show signs of a "new normal." Kevin was a sign of hope and a new beginning.

It was a change to date someone. I struggled and my friends struggled; we had all spent so much time together over the past year, and then there was someone else in my life. When Kevin and I first started dating, I did not want to be "tied down" to a guy after I had spent a year being "tied down" with a back problem. He understood that, and in the beginning our relationship was on my terms. We saw each other when I wanted to and he carefully allowed me to spend time with my friends as well. But any one-sided relationship is not healthy, and we were able to work through that.

Eventually I wanted to spend more time with him and less time with my friends. I was slowly in the process of pushing aside all reminders of the accident. As I continued to heal physically and emotionally, I tried to ignore the accident as much as I could. Kevin allowed me to do that. I am sure it was easier for him to spend time with someone who was not always so engrossed in sorrow. My happiness that semester carried me through the sadness and through our summer apart.

The summer between my sophomore and junior years, Lorrei lived with my family in Phoenix. She became a part of our family that summer. I did not know it at the time, but she and I would have some rocky times ahead, perhaps from too much togetherness. Our time together that summer added to a foundation that would never crack. I had been cleared by Dr. Garfin to begin training again and I wanted her to train with me. I did not want to be alone.

Lorrei and I swam and life-guarded, and I wrote letters to Kevin. I am sure that annoyed her. How could it not? She spent a year, a really rough year, faithfully by my side. And once I was "healed" and started feeling better, I spent all my free time with a new boyfriend. Subconsciously I was trying to escape my past, but it was not fair of me. I was not fair to her. Our friendship deserved more than that, and thankfully, our friendship survived this strain.

At the end of the summer, Lorrei spent some time at home and my family vacationed in Hawaii, my destination of choice. While no one complained about the holiday, the Scott family still lived in our Haley-centric world and we went where I wanted to go; just like we ate where I wanted to eat and we did what I wanted to do. I am not sure that was right, but that was how it was. My parents might have rethought the decision to go to Hawaii had they known I would go jet skiing.

That summer, two years post-op, Dr. Garfin had cleared me for any activity.

"Anything?" I asked gleefully.

"Anything. Well, probably not bungee jumping." He smiled.

But I took "anything" to heart and I went jet skiing in Hawaii with my brother. On the beach, it made my mother physically ill to watch me bounce around on a jet ski. My parents were livid with my brother.

"But she was driving!" He pleaded.

It did not matter. To them, it was his fault—it couldn't be mine.

And it did not matter anyway because I was fine. I had fun, and for the first time in over two years, I felt carefree in the water. How could that be harmful?

When we returned to Notre Dame to begin our junior year, Lorrei, Amy Bethem and I roomed together in Lyons Hall. I was thrilled to be back on campus, back with Kevin, but I had only one thing on my mind: swimming. More specifically, swimming on October 29 at the Midwestern Collegiate Conference (MCC) dual meet at Rolfs Aquatic Center. My first meet.

The first two months of school, my entire focus was on that meet. In September, the crew from ESPN visited for a 6 a.m. interview at the pool. Yes, 6 a.m.! I had always liked Steve Cyphers and the rest of the guys from ESPN. They were nice, funny, very knowledgeable and professional. Some reporters who interviewed me knew very little about my injury and recovery, let alone the sport of swimming. But Steve had followed my story for 20 months; he knew me well and it was evident in his interview.

Most importantly, on a personal level, Mr. Cyphers was extremely respectful and sensitive to my life and my feelings. He came for an interview in September, instead of closer to the meet in October, because in four weeks I would be studying for midterms and focusing on my race. While he would return to campus to film the meet, the bulk of the interview was done when I was less distracted and could give him my undivided time. I always felt very lucky and appreciative of the media's careful handling of my story. Even though I did not like the one time I cried in front of the camera, I never felt pressured or invaded by the press.

It was hard not to think about the MCC meet, but thinking about it made me nervous. I was nervous and excited. I loved training and I loved being back on the team, though to them I had been all along. But despite training hard, I did not feel fast. I did not feel like I had that quick speed that it takes to win a race. I tried to tell myself that it was not about winning, but I was desperate to be as good as I was before. And "before," quite often, meant winning.

Part of me was afraid I might make a fool of myself in competition. No one else would perceive it that way, but I worried about it nonetheless. One day in early October, the team swam time trials—racing, but the only competition was ourselves—and my times were slow. I was sad. There were only 21 days until my first meet and the clock was ticking faster than the stopwatch when I swam. What was worse than swimming slow, however, was how everyone told me how great I was doing. Please. I was slow, not great. They were trying to help and be supportive, although I know they truly believed my efforts were great. But I knew better, or I felt differently. I was my harshest critic and I knew I was not fast.

Thank goodness I was able to go home for part of Fall Break, the week before the MCC meet. Like any college student who had just taken midterm exams, I was tired. I still had trouble concentrating in class and handling the self-imposed pressure of doing well in school. I wanted to be normal, but the reality was my body was not. The combination of swimming, taking five classes and trying to establish some sort of a social life was draining. My mom sensed this and often asked me what I did with my free time.

"Sleep."

I do not think she believed me until I came home for Fall Break and slept for three days. As much as I loved it, it was still really hard to be at school. Home was relaxing, without school work and without feeling like the focus was entirely on me. But that was not true; in fact, it was quite the opposite. But at least at home I did not have to pretend I was not nervous. With one week until the swim meet, I was nervous, excited and scared.

When I returned to Notre Dame, the campus was quiet. Most students had not returned from Fall Break, including my roommates, Lorrei and Amy. It was nice to have some time to myself in our dorm room. And I decided for my senior year that I would live in a single. Alone would be good.

While at home and then back at school, I decided to drop American Government from that semester's class load. Five classes had been too ambitious, too overwhelming, at least for me. But it meant I would be at Notre Dame for five years, or at least an extra semester. There was no way I would be able to make up the classes I had missed by attending summer school. And realistically, summer school was not an option. I knew that come May, I would be ready to leave again, ready for a break at home, even though it was hard to be there too. Being in Phoenix was difficult and being at school was difficult. What I did not fully recognize at the time was that this had nothing to do with the locations. It had nothing to do with my mother being overprotective. Nor did it have anything to do with the demands of being at school. Home and Notre Dame did not cause my difficulties; the events surrounding the accident made my life difficult. But that was hard to acknowledge because I tried to pretend I was able to move on.

With one less class to worry about, I was able to focus on the big event. The day for which I had waited and dreamed for 21 months. My one goal. The light at the end of a dark night. I was so excited and so nervous that I tried to think of anything else to keep it off my mind. But I could not. It was time.

21

Thursday, October 28, 1993

My first race is not a one-day event. It is a weekend-long affair that begins with a press conference in the morning, the day before the meet. I walk through the main entrance of Rolfs Aquatic Center and I am greeted by signs that read "Haley Scott Press Conference This Way" with an arrow. I feel both embarrassed and nervous. It hits me that this is a really big deal, and not just to me. When I arrive in the team classroom overlooking the pool, there are about 20 people waiting: the local Big-3 affiliates, CNN and ESPN; each with their own cameras and their own reporters. Most of them I have met before. They are familiar faces and all of them are extremely gracious.

With the lights on and the cameras and tape recorders set, the questions begin. I am asked these same questions almost daily, so I barely have to think before I respond as I am well-rehearsed.

"How do you feel?"

"I am really excited to wear my Notre Dame swim cap and compete again for the Fighting Irish."

"Are you nervous?"

"A little bit, but I know once I am on the starting block and I hear the beep, it will all seem natural and come back to me."

"What events are you swimming tomorrow?"

"The 50- and 100-yard freestyle and the 100-yard butterfly."

"How do you think your teammates will feel racing against you?"

This is the only question that catches me off guard. But it is still an easy one.

"I know all my teammates wish me well and are excited for me, especially Meghan and Colleen. They are the reason I am swimming."

It is the first time I am able to talk about Meghan and Colleen and not worry about the tears. Not today. I am too excited.

We exchange thank yous and I am wished good luck by everyone in the room. This is their triumph too. I am a child of Notre Dame and of the South Bend community. Even as unbiased and objective reporters, they have been rooting for this comeback and cheering me on. I did not seek them out, yet I am hesitant to turn them down. The people who carried me on this journey deserve to witness the fruit of their prayers and to know how much I appreciate their love.

I arrive in the morning for warm-ups to find a pool in chaos. For a swim meet at Notre Dame, which is usually only sparsely attended by visiting parents, it is crowded on the pool deck and packed upstairs in the seating galley. Wow! I am surprised. My mom gives me a hug and whispers, "They are all here to see you."

I am doubtful, but she believes it. And it is true that I have never seen this many people here for a swim meet. A banner hangs from the balcony. I look up and see my brother standing behind it. "Of course," I think. "Of course he would do that."

"From a wiggle to a step to a flip turn, the miracle continues: GO HALEY!"

My brother smiles and waves, and I cannot help but smile back. It is a little embarrassing, as I do not like attention. But he is just that proud.

I warm up in the same way I have before at dozens of meets. So far everything is familiar and routine: stretching, a warm-up swim, and practice sprints before the race. Then my favorite: the team prayer and cheer. There is a buzz at the pool. It might be all the people or it might be the trail of photographers following me around. Some are here for the first time and some, like my friend Ed Ballotts from the *South Bend Tribune*, have taken this journey with me. There are cameras everywhere, watching. They watch as I warm up, as I sit by myself and listen to my walkman, and as I approach the starting blocks when my first event is announced: the 50-yard freestyle. Meghan's event.

As I make my way across the bulkhead to lane three, I am keenly aware of the crowd. I try not to look at my teammates or upstairs at my family. I know they are all there: my mom, my dad, my brother, my aunt and uncle and my cousin. But I need to focus. This is it.

Part of me thought it would be the same as every other race, but it is not. Part of me knew it would be different, but it is not. I am strangely comfortable and uncomfortable at the same time.

As the swimmer from the heat prior to mine gets out of lane three, she gives me a hug and says, "Good luck!" Again, I am surprised and not surprised by her kindness and sportsmanship.

Going through the heat sheet, the announcer calls out, "Swimming in lane number three, Haley Scott of Notre Dame!"

The pool erupts. Everyone cheers and I cannot help but smile and acknowledge their love. Their cheers contrast loudly with the silent prayers many of them once said. But I am still unable to look up and find my parents; I have to keep my emotions in check. I have to focus. This is it. This is it. Deep breath. I step up on the starting block, stand up straight and look down toward the end of the pool. The 50-yard freestyle. Down and back. Two laps, one flip turn. I take another deep breath and shake my arms at the side of my body. This is an old habit. It's back. I'm back.

"Swimmers take your marks!"

I bend down and grab the edge of the starting block. My back is fused in a place that does not normally bend. How fortunate to break my back and still be able to touch my toes. I am free to bend over and…

The shrill starting horn blares!

My instincts and reflexes are still intact. I leap off the starting block, dive into the cool water, and begin to kick. The muscles in my legs respond to propel my body forward as it glides to the surface. The strokes come quickly and I concentrate on staying smooth and not rushing my arms. As I approach the wall to make the flip turn I take my first breath, yet remain completely unaware of the celebration above. The entire aquatic center is watching in anticipation, some cheering, some holding their breath. But I am focused only on the water and the black cross marking the wall as I somersault to make my turn. My legs power me off the wall and I am in the home stretch. In this race, the flip turn is the middle of two distinct parts of the race. For a swimmer, the first lap of a sprint is easy and quick, energized and smooth. In the second lap we find ourselves more tired and fatigued. But we reach deep within and find the strength to persevere and finish the race.

I touch the timing pad on the wall and turn around to look at the scoreboard.

First place: lane three.

I look around. I am in lane three. Is this even possible? I take my goggles off to make sure. First place: lane three. 25.04 seconds. I catch my breath and know that now I can look up in the stands. Only then do I realize the crowd is going crazy. People are jumping up and down, yelling, cheering, clapping and crying. Finally, I look to find my mom and see both her arms outstretched in the air. I smile and give my family a little wave.

That's it. I did it. I climb out of the pool and cross the bulkhead to a waiting mob of photographers and reporters. It is a mob. Cameras click and microphones hang over my head from afar to record anything I might say.

I see Coach Tim first. We hug and I barely hear what he says. The pool is so loud with cheers and his voice is held back by emotion, but I know what he is feeling and his hug is enough. There are more hugs from my teammates: Amy, with red soaked eyes, Lorrei, Angie, Cara and Jenni. They are all there, they were all watching. No other Notre Dame swimmer was in my heat. I did not have to compete against a teammate in my first swim. They were able to watch and enjoy what they had prayed for and waited for 21 months.

After a quick warm down swim and many congratulating words from other teams, I put on my "ND Swimming" sweats and notice the black arm band stitched around the upper part of the sleeve. It was added during our freshman year; only the members of the 1991-92 swim team continue to wear it. It is our badge of honor. I touch it gently, close my eyes, and whisper, "Thank you."

While the swim meet continues in the pool and for those on deck, the celebration continues upstairs in the spectators' galley. I see my dad first. There is no need for words, a hug is enough.

Hugs, hugs and more hugs. Mom, Stephen, Aunt Barbara, Uncle Gary, my cousin Tiffany, and many of my teammates' parents. Kevin Kubsch, the trooper who was first on the scene of the accident has come to watch. So has Dr. Halperin, my Emergency Room doctor at Memorial. Notre Dame's basketball coach, John MacLeod, and some of his players stopped in on their way back from practice. Sister Kathleen, students, professors—the Notre Dame family has come out in full force, even during Fall Break, a vacation week at school.

My mom tells me there is one more person I need to see. She was not sure she would be able to come, but after celebrating what would have been her daughter's 21st birthday the day before, Ann Hipp knew where she needed to be. She knew Colleen would have wanted her here. When she woke up this morning, Mrs. Hipp got in her car and drove six hours from St. Louis to South Bend.

I slowly make my way over to this woman who I have only met once, yet to whom I feel a deep connection. She is wearing one of Colleen's t-shirts: a short-sleeved, royal blue shirt that reads "Irish '91" in yellow on the front. We embrace without words and hug for what seems like minutes. Neither of us wants to let go. For the first time on this emotional day, I cry. I can no longer hold it in. When it comes to Colleen and Meghan, there are no walls.

Mrs. Hipp has brought her own sign. It is a poster board with a map of the United States. On it are two angels, my two angels, our two angels: Colleen and Meghan.

The other two events I swim that day, the 100-yard freestyle and the 100-yard butterfly, are exciting but uneventful. Nothing will ever be like that first race. I am asked to attend a press conference between the morning preliminary session and the afternoon finals session. It is attended by most of the same news affiliates and reporters as the day before. My parents sit on either side of me. My hair is wet and I wear my team sweats. We are in the pressroom that the football team and other more popular sports use. I imagine this is the first time a swimmer has held court. After the precursory, yet sincere, congratulations, the questions are first directed toward my parents.

My mom, always composed, says, "The best part about today was just being a mom, and getting to see your daughter swim again." She is wearing what she calls her "Notre Dame dress." It is a blue and gold plaid dress that she saves for events that she attends with me. It is her Dress Code A.

My dad, not always comfortable with his emotions, turns to

humor: "I'm just glad she didn't false-start!" He always has a way of making me smile.

My own comments are few, and only one makes the rounds on the news that night, "I used to think my first race would signify the end of my recovery, but really it's just the beginning of the rest of my swimming career."

In truth, it was both.

22

The days following the swim meet were like "Parade of Flowers" Part II. The cards, flowers and even a few plants arrived all week. With the story covered on CNN and ESPN, people countrywide heard about my return to swimming. They celebrated as I did. Many of them took the time to write and congratulate me. I was touched. If only they each knew how much their cards and flowers meant to me. It had been almost two years and everyone was still so caring and so concerned. I wanted to write back to each of them to thank them, but I was still trying hard to focus on school.

The phone rang constantly, and I took to not answering it. My roommate and teammate, Amy, was happy to do so for me. She enjoyed taking messages and writing down the names of television movie producers who called with interest in making a TV movie. I remember one phone call in particular, because it was so distinctive and humorous.

"Hi, this is Rudy. From the movie *Rudy!*"

My dad met with a producer from the movie *Rudy* and several other producers as well over the next few months. But ultimately, I decided not to do it. I was not ready to be the movie of the week, and I was correct in my instincts. I would learn years later that my story did not end with my first race in October 1993. It would be a life-long journey. With my physical recovery complete, my "real" education—the personal, emotional and spiritual journey—had just begun.

And I had a lot to learn.

Most Notre Dame football fans recall the 1993 season. We played and defeated the 1990s powerhouse Florida State University in a No. 1 vs. No. 2 matchup. The Fighting Irish were ranked No. 2, but the favored team in this home game. It was billed as the "Game of the Century," and the campus was abuzz with excitement and press.

The pep rally for the "Game of the Century" was held one week after my first race, on the Friday night before the football game. The basketball arena overflowed with fans and students. We had a swim meet that afternoon and most swimmers rushed through warm-down, barely showering, to sneak through the back door to the floor of arena. I asked Coach if I could skip the last relay. I had a speech to write.

I too walked through the back corridors of the Joyce Center, from the pool to the basketball arena. But I was stopped in the hall-way and told to wait with the football players, who were lined up to parade into the pep rally. Standing there between two much larger student-athletes, I heard the buzz:

"Who's the speaker?"

"I hear it's Joe Montana!"

"Oh, that's awesome!"

I wanted to disappear into the wall I was leaning against.

"Maybe it's Regis!"

"It better be somebody good. This is a big game!"

It was then, I think, that they noticed there was a female stand-ing among them. I do not know if they knew who I was, but I would guess some of them did. I smiled and said, "It's just me."

Thankfully one of the players, who it was I cannot recall, replied without hesitation, "It *is* someone good. That's awesome."

Maybe he felt sorry for me, or maybe he was sincere. It did not matter. His words put me at ease. I was relaxed and ready to go. If the football players were not disappointed with me as their speaker, then I would not disappoint the crowd either.

It was a thrill for me to walk into the gym between the football players and their coach, Lou Holtz. The lights were out, so I walked carefully to my seat in the front row next to the coaches. I could see the swim team sitting close on the floor.

Most of the pep rally was a blur; I only spoke for two minutes, but that was enough. I talked about how Notre Dame athletes spe-cialize in beating the odds, as I had done and as our football team would do the following day. But what I remember most clearly was Coach Holtz presenting me with the previous game's game ball, a tradition that takes place with each victory. The football was inscribed with my name, the date, the opponent and the score of the game. I received the Notre Dame vs. Navy game ball to commemorate the weekend of my first race. I still have the ball displayed in my home in Annapolis, Maryland, just five miles from the United States Naval Academy.

The next day, the football team did beat the odds. They defeated top-ranked Florida State by a score of 31-24.

I continued swimming for Notre Dame through my junior and senior years. But I never swam faster than I did at that first meet. My time in the 50-yard freestyle with my family, friends and the cameras watching was the fastest I would ever swim again. I was satisfied with my times during my junior year, still riding high from being back on the team. But after training hard the summer before my senior year, it was defeating to not improve my times. I was able to train with my teammates; I just could not keep up with the competition at the collegiate level. Recently, I reread the article from the *South Bend Tribune* where a doctor stated that I might never compete again at the same level. He was right. I had wanted so badly for him to be wrong, and perhaps his statement gave me motivation to push forward.

At the beginning of the second semester of my senior year, I sat down with Coach Tim Welsh to talk about my last few months of swimming. I had an additional year of eligibility left, and I would be staying an extra semester to complete my course work. But I knew I was done. Tim knew how hard this was for me. He could see it in my eyes each time I raced and each time I looked at the clock when I finished. He tried to stay positive, and he had every right to be. I was swimming. I wasn't even supposed to walk, and I was swimming.

But that was not enough for me. I wanted to be good. I wanted to be great. The competitor in me that gave me the will and the drive to make it to this point, also caused me to feel defeated when I came to recognize my limitations. I had never felt limited in my life and it was humbling. Even when I was told I would not walk, I knew I would. But after two years of trying to improve my times, I was faced with limitations my body could not overcome. And I had to be okay with that.

I focused on the healing, and not on my perceived failings. I would never be the swimmer, just as I would never be the person I was before the accident. I came out of it a better person, though not a better swimmer. It was a valuable, but hard lesson to learn, and one for which I am grateful. Swimming competitively would end with my college diploma, but being a better person was a life-long process and a continuous goal.

Coach Tim and I agreed that I would swim only relays for the remainder of the season, no individual events. I could not quit the team. If I believed in quitting, I would have quit. But I did not, even though it was that hard to be there. Some girls did decide to leave the team; that was what was best for them and I never judged them for their decision. It just was not for me.

So my swimming career ended as it began: relatively uneventful. By swimming on relays I felt as though I was contributing to the team without the clock and my times glaring at me. My parents found my last meet much less entertaining, and unknowingly went for a walk during my last event. They missed my last race at Notre Dame. In my deepest depression, I wanted to lash out at my mom and tell her that she only watched me swim when the cameras were there. But that was not true; it was just my anger speaking. What I came to learn was that it was too hard for her to be there. As difficult as it was for me, it was just as painful for her to know how unhappy her daughter was while doing something that she loved. After everything I had been through, my mom felt I deserved a little happiness. What I did not appreciate at the time was that she did too.

Thankfully and when we looked for it, my mom and I both found that we were surrounded by happiness. We just had to open our eyes beyond ourselves to see it. We were both surrounded by a support group and emotional network that was tied to my story and my swimming career. I was "Haley Scott, Notre Dame Swimmer" and she was "Haley's mom" or "Delicious" to those who remembered her apple outfit from the hospital. These were titles in which we took great pride, though for me it sometimes carried the responsibility of being singled out.

I won several awards during my last two years at Notre Dame, some local, some national, and all meaningful. Each award reminded me to be proud of what I had accomplished, to be happy with all I had achieved and to celebrate the small victories in life, even though they might not be the ones I wanted to win.

These awards also introduced me to some fascinating people whom I never would have met otherwise. Orville Redenbacher and I were the recipients of the Michiana Executive Journal Award. I had the privilege, much to my dad's thrill, of meeting Gene Autry as a recipient of the inaugural Gene Autry Courage in Sport Award in 1994. And coming full circle, I was presented with the Honda Award for Inspiration at the Honda Awards Program, a celebration of women's athletics, at the NCAA convention in San Diego in January 1995. My parents invited Dr. and Mrs. Garfin to be our guests at the awards dinner, and we shared the evening with Missy Conboy and Dick Rosenthal.

Sitting on the dais with me were several standout college athletes: soccer phenomenon Mia Hamm, basketball player Lisa Leslie, swimmer Nicole Haislett, volleyball player Danielle Scott and softball pitcher Susie Parra. I was humbled to be in their presence. And 18 months later, while watching the Summer Olympic Games in Atlanta, I marveled at their Olympic feats. Was I worthy to be with them on that stage? Maybe not in athletic talent, but I was learning I had an Olympic-sized inspirational story.

I "walked" with my Notre Dame graduating class in May 1995, knowing I would return in the fall to complete my three remaining classes. There was a ceremony that weekend in the rotunda of the Main Building, beneath the Golden Dome, awarding Meghan Beeler and Colleen Hipp their degrees posthumously. It was a bittersweet weekend. I said goodbye to my friends while looking forward to returning to campus for one more semester. It was that day that I realized I had made the right decision. Saying goodbye to Lorrei, Amy, Angie and the rest of my classmates and teammates was hard enough. I was glad I did not have to say goodbye to Notre Dame as well.

During the summer of 1995, the University split the men's and women's programs. Our assistant coach, Randy Julian, left Notre Dame to take the head-coaching position at Bowling Green

University. Tim Welsh became head coach of the Notre Dame men's swim team, and a new women's coach was hired. It needed to be done. No nationally ranked program shared a coach for both the men's and the women's teams, but it was strange to have a new women's head coach while I was still a student. But that was exactly the case: with the exception of me, our class had graduated. Out of respect for our class, the teams had remained united through our four years. The University did what they felt was best for us. They were right. Then they did what was best for the swim programs. They were right again. As student-athletes, our well-being always came first.

My extra semester gave me time to separate from a place that had so defined my life. I never second-guessed my decision to stay, just as I never second-guessed my decision to not use my last year of swimming eligibility, though I often spent time at the pool and with the younger swimmers. My childhood friend Nancy, who had graduated that May from St. Mary's College, stayed in South Bend as well. She married a Notre Dame graduate student that fall, and we shared an off-campus apartment. Once Nancy got married, I was completely on my own for the first time at age 22. No mother, no Sister Kathleen, no roommate. I enjoyed it most of the time, but it also forced me to deal with my future and my past, without influences or distractions.

With only three classes and no athletic commitments, I was offered an unpaid internship with Missy Conboy in the Athletic Department.

A former basketball player and NCAA administrator, Missy was and is a role model for all women athletes at Notre Dame, myself included. Working for her was an honor. I wrote memos, answered e-mails and had the opportunity to observe the day-to-day operations of a Division I athletic department. I would have loved to have continued along that path by working in an athletic department at a university. I had always enjoyed college sports, and Missy was helpful in sharing with me job opportunities within the industry. But I needed to go home. Four years after the bus accident, my emotions were still too raw. I needed to leave, to find myself and to heal before I could return to campus feeling only joy.

23

I said goodbye to Notre Dame in January 1996, and moved back to Phoenix. I had plans to teach and coach at my high school alma mater, Xavier College Preparatory, in the fall—eight months away. But until then, I had some work to do.

I made one last medical visit to Dr. Garfin. In March 1996, I returned to San Diego and the Ritz Carlton of hospitals, Thorton Hospital, to have the Edwards rods removed. They were large, close to the surface, and painful when I leaned back in a chair. My spine had fused solid, and the rods were no longer needed for support. I was slightly frightened to undergo surgery again. As fearless as I had been at 18 years old, I knew better this time at age 22. Things can go wrong. Surgery hurts. But time heals and had allowed me to forget most of the horror. It had been nearly four years since my past operations in San Diego, and while there is always risk, this back surgery would be nothing compared to what I went through before.

The rod removal went well. It was relatively painless, as Dr. Garfin said it would be, and for the first time, my recovery required no rehab. There was no loss of function or strength to regain.

Once the incision on my back healed, I was much more comfortable. The surgery was actually harder for Dr. Garfin than it was for me. My bones had fused solid—thank goodness—which meant the bone had grown around the rods as well. This required Dr. Garfin to chip away at this area to dislodge the rods. I asked several times if I could keep the metal instrumentation, and when I woke up from the three-hour operation, the rods were sitting in a sterile urine specimen-type cup, labeled "SAVE FOR PATIENT." They were larger in diameter than I thought they would be, but they were also cut into two- to three-inch pieces, which had been necessary in order for Dr. Garfin to remove them. I would later tie each piece of metal to a string to make a wind chime. Believe it or not, they make a pretty chiming sound.

This was also the first time I talked to Dr. Garfin about my bladder. I had never mentioned it before because he was more concerned with the bigger picture: straightening my back and preventing further damage to my spinal cord. While my back had healed as well as possible, I still suffered from nerve damage that at this time would remain permanent. Compared to the obvious, some of this nerve damage was minor: some leg and feet numbness, poor balance and a diminished sense of proprioception, the ability to know where my feet are without looking at them. Maybe not minor to another 22-year-old, but certainly minor to me.

But my neurogenic bladder, its official diagnosis, was a quality of life issue. A daily, even hourly issue. And one that, thankfully, could be helped.

In the hospital in South Bend, I remember Nurse Debbie telling me that if I was unable to void on my own, I would have to catheterize myself for the rest of my life. I thought that sounded horrible. So horrible, in fact, that I used it as motivation to regain function within a matter of days. Four years later, intermittent catheterization, along with medication, was a huge blessing. I could now go for hours without using the restroom; I could exercise without bathroom trips; I could go shopping without knowingly staying close to the ladies room. The once dreaded diagnosis had changed my life.

Always looking out for me, Dr. Garfin did his best to minimize the scar tissue on my back. For a 12-inch long incision that had been cut five times, the skin was badly damaged. Dr. Garfin removed this scar tissue and stitched me up from the inside. "I'm not a plastic surgeon, but your scar will look a lot nicer."

He did not have to do that, but when I danced with him at my wedding, wearing a strapless wedding gown, I thanked him.

My parents stayed and I recovered at a condo on San Diego's Mission Beach that belonged to the Thomas family, friends from Phoenix. Once again, I was blessed and touched by the generosity of the human spirit. How could I repay so many people? I could not, I decided. I just need to pass it along and be that generous person when others are in need.

In the future I will frequently hear how thoughtful or how helpful I am, and people thank me for it. What they do not realize is that

I am just paying back the kindness I received for the many years I needed it. I still need it. And people are still kind.

1996 was an Olympic year, just as 1992, the year of the accident, had been; yet the two Olympic years could not have contrasted more. I had the opportunity to participate in a small but extremely meaningful way in the preparation of the Summer Games in Atlanta.

My sister-in-law Marcia nominated me to carry the Olympic Torch, and I was selected to take part in the Phoenix leg of the Relay Across America. I carried the eternal Olympic flame with as much pride as if I was an Olympic athlete competing that summer. Three months later, I cried as I watched Muhammad Ali light the cauldron in Atlanta with the same Olympic flame I had carried. We were all athletes in the sport of life, and I had won my gold medal.

My sister-in-law was also responsible for another treasured journey. While visiting my brother and her at their home in Atlanta, Marcia's company sponsored a charity event to raise money for a therapeutic riding center. Christopher Reeve was the guest of honor. I had followed his story closely after his May 1995 accident, and took great interest in his medical advancements. There were very few people who understood what it took for him just to leave his house. He was courageous beyond words. Marcia and I flew on a private plane to pick up Mr. Reeve and his entourage in White Plains, New York. We then had the privilege to serve as his flight attendants on our way back to Atlanta. It was a thrill just to meet him. I got to fly with Superman!

In the five years following college, I worked at my alma mater, Xavier College Preparatory, as a History teacher and swim coach, and eventually a position for which I did not interview: Assistant Dean of Students. With this role came the responsibility and privilege of being co-Moderator for the Senior Class Student Council.

I loved teaching World Cultures and U.S. History. It was a lot of work, but it was also rewarding, entertaining and educational. I learned as much in my four years as a teacher at Xavier as I did when I was a student there. They were different lessons: less academic and more personal and spiritual.

Working at a Catholic high school and the community it provided, reconfirmed my decision to officially join the Catholic

Church. I had been raised a Christian mutt: I was baptized Presbyterian, spent my elementary school years attending an Episcopal Church, my junior high years in the Methodist Church and finally I studied in high school and college at Catholic institutions. Same God, same Jesus. But only in the Catholic Church did I find the comfort and the spiritual home I was seeking. For others it is elsewhere. But for me, my life had been so definitively defined by the accident. At a time when I had nothing to turn to but faith and God, it was the Catholic Church that embraced me, a non-Catholic, and showed me how to truly believe. It was a life changing and life-long gift for which I am truly grateful.

As I grew spiritually and through prayer, I also found a new respect for my body, for what it had done and what it was capable of doing. Without the daily reminder and disappointment of swimming slowly, I was able to marvel at how well my body had healed and to celebrate the miracle of its recovery. I also set upon it some new challenges.

A friend from Xavier, Ellie, and I decided to run a marathon. It was a challenge and a form of therapy for both of us; for her because she had just lost her father, and for me because I was still sorting through my own emotions. For four months we ran daily, talking through our emotional journeys and working our way toward the Los Angeles Marathon in March 1997. As we crossed the finish line, we celebrated a reaffirmation of life in many ways.

The following year, I took on a different feat: the Mrs. T's Triathlon in Chicago. A former Notre Dame teammate and a future professional triathlete, Linda convinced me that we would have an edge in the mile swim because we were former swimmers. Having run a marathon, I did not think the 10K run would be difficult. And the biking portion was around 25 miles. How hard could that be? Very hard when you do not use your own bike and you are unable to raise the seat! After my mile swim in Lake Michigan, I peddled up and down Michigan Avenue with my knees in my chest, watching most of the competition ride by. So much for an edge in the water; I needed a bike that fit. But it was fun, and again I finished without worrying about my time or place. More importantly I was learning to love competition again, to love training and to love the companionship of sport.

As Assistant Dean of Students at Xavier, I watched an incredible mentor shape the moral lives of young women. Dean Noreen Reed demanded honesty and respect, and enforced discipline with as much consistency as possible. Yet as tough as she was, she was loved by the students. I learned quickly that as a young teacher it is easy to be liked, but it is critical to be respected. Noreen was the epitome of this, and despite our 30-year age difference, we shared a unique and equal friendship. We shared many laughs, as high school girls can be unendingly entertaining; and we also shared many tears.

As senior class co-moderator and Assistant Dean of Students, I was responsible for chaperoning the Junior-Senior Prom. That night, usually a highlight in the life of a high school girl, Xavier lost one of its best students. Emily was one of our senior class officers. She was a member of Xavier's state championship golf team and an all-around kind person. Alcohol took her life as she pulled out of the hotel leaving her senior prom. She and her date had not been drinking. Instead, her car was hit by a 50-year-old drunk driver, who himself had an 18-year-old daughter attending her own prom that year. Emily died hours later.

The events of that night and the next several days were similar to what I imagined Notre Dame to be in the days following the bus accident. As I navigated my way through a memorial service at Xavier, walked the halls of a campus in shock and mourning, and attended Emily's funeral, I could not help but reflect on what those days and weeks at Notre Dame must have been like. I was not there when it happened; I was in the hospital unable to move. When it happened at Xavier, I relived my accident all over again.

Emily's mom had always been a presence at Xavier. She was constantly involved in the Mothers' Guild (Xavier's PTA) and supported the school in all areas. When she spoke so eloquently—so amazingly for a woman who had just lost her daughter—at Xavier's annual "moving up Mass" on Ascension Thursday, she said something that struck and stuck with me.

"My husband finally understands why I spend so much time

here. Because this is my family and we are both overwhelmed by the support we have received from the Xavier community."

I knew how she felt, in my own way. I could never understand the devastation of losing a child, and I hope I never do. But I could understand the sense of comfort and support that the Catholic and Christian community provided. I had felt it myself. Not only had I been a part of Notre Dame's community, but Xavier's as well. I realized then that I had left one secure and supportive campus to return to another. But what was my role in this new community? How was I doing my part to be supportive? These were questions I constantly found myself asking and trying to answer. Once again recognizing that I could never repay the generosity of the human spirit, I was reminded that I had to pass it on.

I wondered how to help this family who was suffering. Could I help them? And then I knew. Going through the motions of the last month of school was the rest of the senior class and my senior class officers. I could not stop thinking about them. They too lost a friend and classmate needlessly at 18 years old. I did not know what Emily's family was going through, but I knew what her friends were going through. With only a month left before graduation, I felt it was okay to get personal. I could be their friend and not just their teacher. I reached out to some of the seniors, to some of Emily's friends, and I shared with them my loss of Meghan and Colleen. It was painful for me, yet healing at the same time. Some students opened up, some did not. But knowing that I reached one or two was enough. It eased my hurt to comfort them. I spent hours in Xavier's Chapel listening to the myriad of emotions that I knew so well. And I could say honestly, as not many could, "I understand what you are going through."

Perhaps this was my role in this community. Perhaps this was what brought me back to Xavier: to learn, as I did, from Noreen; and to teach, as I did, historical and life lessons to my students.

I knew this was what I wanted for my life and in my life: this community, this sense of belonging. For as independent as I thought I was, I needed to learn that I was part of something bigger than myself. I needed to step out of the ego-centric world in which I had lived for so long and function independently, but as part of a greater unit. It was only when I came to this realization that I was able to function in a healthy relationship with a man.

Jamie DeMaria, our swim team manager from Notre Dame, was with me the night Emily was killed. He was in graduate school at Florida State University, but had flown to Arizona to be my prom date. As we took our prom picture inside at the end of the dance, the event that changed the course of our relationship happened outside. Jamie stood by me that night as we watched while Emily was taken away. He comforted me at the hospital when we learned she had died. He went home with me that night as I cried for the loss of an innocent life, and for the loss of Meghan and Colleen. And he was there for me over the next several weeks, giving me the support I needed to be able to help Emily's friends.

That summer it hit me. Jamie was someone who would be here for me, who would support me in bad times, who would comfort me and celebrate and laugh with me. Being with Jamie was my first conscious step in creating a community, a life, where I could contribute, and where I knew I would be okay.

Less than two years later, we were married. The Notre Dame community showed up in full force: former teammates, coaches and Missy Conboy attended; one of my history professors, Father Blantz, married us. For Jamie and me it was a celebration of love and the beginning of a new life together in a new city. For my parents it was a celebration of love and letting go. They were happy that I was happy, but they still worried about the one looming uncertainty as to whether or not I would be able to have children.

On January 23, 2002, one day shy of the 10-year anniversary of the bus accident, I gave birth to our first son, James. Two years later, Edward was born. My life was complete. I was healed. I was not "normal," but I no longer wanted to be.

It took me several years to understand that the bus accident changed my life forever. I will never be the same person. I suffered and struggled, and I learned that change is not always a bad thing. I am stronger and more sensitive. I am more aware of others and I have learned to care for them beyond my own needs. I feel emotions at a deeper level and I find myself reaching out to others. I like being that person.

When I see an accident or a tragedy on television, I know what it is like to be that news story. It is more than a two-minute story. Tragedy affects the lives of those involved and those who love them, and it changes them forever. The challenge is to survive and accept and embrace the change in order to find meaning in the illness, or death, or injury, or in whatever way your life has been altered.

If I had waited for my life to return to normal, I would still be waiting. My story has not ended; it lives on in the beating hearts of all of us inextricably intertwined from that night of horror and tragedy, and in the families and friends of those we lost. I carry this with me every single day, as do the rest of us who have survived their own tragedies. Life is a river that eventually takes us to God's own sea, and I think all He expects from us is to honor Him in victory and defeat. We are not in control; He is. And when one of us is lost, we mourn and move forward, knowing that today is only what we make it to be, and tomorrow is never promised. I thank God for each and every day.

As I look back I can reflect on how all my relationships were challenged and changed. Any relationship prior to the bus accident either disappeared or had to be redefined. Friends from high school whose friendships with me survived, and there were not many—Nancy and Maren—had to endure my distance at times. But they chose to stick with me.

Often times they were the recipients of my anger, but they were faithful and steadfast in their loyalty. In many ways, they have been better friends to me than I to them. Thankfully, I was able to recognize and acknowledge this, and they have forgiven me. I will spend a lifetime grateful for their unwavering friendship, and hopefully I add to the fullness of their lives as well.

My relationship with my family was ever-evolving, as each of us spent years trying to navigate the new directions in which the accident sent our lives.

My brother and I continued to grow closer as our lives began to parallel. He got married and had children; I got married and had children. We always shared the bond we formed, like all others who were there, in the hospital in South Bend. Several years later, unbeknownst to me, Stephen was inspired by my LA Marathon poster to run a marathon himself. He never told me, until after he crossed the finish line, that he had trained every day for six months, wearing only Notre Dame clothing in my honor.

Following the accident, my relationship with my sister suffered temporarily, in a similar manner to my other close friendships. Until she left for college on a volleyball scholarship at the University of Virginia, she could barely stand to be in the same room as me. And at times I found her equally as difficult. It was painful to be at odds with her, but she needed to escape from my shadow and define her own place in life before she could include me in it. Thankfully she did and we have never been closer.

My relationship with my dad was the one that changed the least. I continued to adore him and he me. I never knew how painful the accident was for him because he never shared it with me, and perhaps he never shared it with himself. But he was one less person with whom I had to talk about it, and for that I think we were both grateful. We never connected on the deep emotional level that my mom and I did, probably because our personalities were so similar. But the love was no less.

My relationship with my mother was ever-evolving, but we have finally found peace: I, with my husband and my children, and she, knowing that I am happy. She still worries about me and I still keep things from her, but less often than I used to. Together we lived through something that most mothers and daughters do not. We are thankful for that; thankful that most women do not have to suffer as we did, and thankful for being able to enjoy the bond that our suffering created.

She always wanted to be my friend, but found it difficult to evolve from her role as my guardian and caretaker. It was a painful break for both of us, but it has allowed us to be friends and has enabled me to turn to her for guidance. I do not think I will ever know or understand what she lived through; but I know above all, she gave me everything she had. And I am who I am today because of her love.

My teammates from college, the ones with whom our lives are

forever linked by the events of the bus accident, are just that: linked. Though time and distance often separate our phone calls or visits, I know if I need them, they will come. And they know I would do the same. They are all accomplished—doctorates, MBAs, master's degrees, mothers, wives and business women. It is amazing how a group of women so devastated by tragedy at such a young age was able to emerge and be successful in all ways that matter. Family. Friendship. Kindness. Our happiness is a testament to our coaches, our school and our families.

There is no way to explain how I feel about these women. The emotions are too deep, ingrained in shared pain, in a friendship that began with such raw emotions that we could not help but love each other. So true, almost prophetic, were the words Coach Tim Welsh spoke at our first swim team meeting: The purpose of Notre Dame Swimming is to pursue athletic excellence with self-discipline and love for one another. I am filled with love.

Acknowledgements

First I must acknowledge the entire 1991-1992 Notre Dame Women's Swim Team and coaches. This too was their bus accident, and their lives and their families' lives were disrupted as well. I especially thank the Beeler and Hipp families, and my dearest friends who lived through their own pain as well as mine: Susan "Scully" Bohdan Walton, Lorrei Horenkamp DiCamillo, Angie Roby Maersch, and Amy Bethem War.

Thank you to Tim Welsh and Randy Julian, our coaches, who delicately and steadfastly ensured our well-being as student-athletes and as young women faced with tragedy.

There are not enough words to thank the University of Notre Dame, although I hope I have been able to convey my deep and eternal gratitude in this book. From the leadership of then-President Father Edward Malloy and then-Athletic Director Dick Rosenthal, to the professors, students and the community at large, I continue to appreciate their unconditional love, support and prayers. Thank you also to Matt Storin, Mike Low and John Heisler for their help in all matters relating to the book.

Thank you to the medical staffs at Memorial Hospital of South Bend and the University of California, San Diego Medical Center. I am testimony to the dedication you show to your profession and patients.

A special thank you to Dr. Steven Garfin and his family.

To Trooper Kevin Kubsch and all those who gave their time, hearts and jackets to us on that fateful night, I thank you.

Thank you to USA Swimming for its continued support and belief in my story. I am indebted to Rick Derby, who painstakingly conducted the interviews that are so vital to the complete perspective of this story, and to those who so generously opened up to him.

Thank you to my friends, Dr. Jeanette White, Susan Walton and Jennie Burke, who spent hours helping to edit and proof the manuscript. Thank you to Gordon Thiessen at Cross Training Publishing for bringing the book to fruition. And to Adam Miller for bringing the book to the public. Certainly not least, I thank co-author Bob Schaller, who gave his expertise and passion to all aspects of this project.

I thank with great love my siblings, Stephen Scott and Mary Frances Cvetas, for their unwavering support; for my brother's encouragement and my sister's willingness to read the manuscript several times. I am inspired by my parents, Steve and Charlotte Scott, for their selflessness in agreeing to relive the accident with me in order to share my story. I could not have written this book without my mother's love and recollections.

To my husband, Jamie, and our two boys, James and Edward: You are my world and the reason I want to make it a better place.

If you prayed for me, I thank you. And I thank God. Keep praying! He listens.

Co-author Bob Schaller thanks his son, Garrett Schaller, Haley Scott DeMaria, her husband Jamie DeMaria, and their extended family for interviews, transcripts and access to very personal information and memories. Read more about Bob's other books at www.BobSchaller.com.

We would also like to thank editors Susan Lang, Ph.D., Brieann Long and Cassie Fasano for their work editing the manuscript.